THE WALKER'S GUIDE TO THE
Castles
OF
Britain

CONWAY
Bloomsbury Publishing Plc
50 Bedford Square, London, WC1B 3DP, UK
29 Earlsfort Terrace, Dublin 2, Ireland

BLOOMSBURY, CONWAY and the Conway logo are trademarks of
Bloomsbury Publishing Plc

First published in Great Britain 2025

Copyright © Julia Goodfellow-Smith, 2025

Julia Goodfellow-Smith has asserted her right under the Copyright, Designs
and Patents Act, 1988, to be identified as Author of this work.

This book is a guide for when you spend time outdoors. Undertaking any activity outdoors carries with it some risks that cannot be entirely eliminated. For example, you might get lost on a route or caught in bad weather. Before you spend time outdoors, we therefore advise that you always take the necessary precautions, such as checking weather forecasts and ensuring that you have all the equipment you need. Any walking routes that are described in this book should not be relied upon as a sole means of navigation, so we recommend that you refer to an Ordnance Survey map or authoritative equivalent.

This book may also reference businesses and venues. Whilst every effort is made by the author and the publisher to ensure the accuracy of the business and venue information contained in our books before they go to print, changes to such information can occur during the production and lifetime of a publication. Therefore, we also advise that you check with businesses or venues for the latest information before setting out.

All internet addresses given in this book were correct at the time of going to press. Bloomsbury Publishing Plc does not have any control over, or responsibility for, any third-party websites referred to or in this book. The author and the publisher regret any inconvenience caused if some facts have changed or sites have ceased to exist, but can accept no responsibility for any such changes.

All rights reserved. No part of this publication may be reproduced or transmitted in any form or by any means, electronic or mechanical, including photocopying, recording, or any information storage or retrieval system, without prior permission in writing from the publishers.

A catalogue record for this book is available from the British Library

Library of Congress Cataloguing-in-Publication data has been applied for

ISBN: PB: 978-1-8448-6646-5; ePub: 978-1-8448-6647-2; ePDF: 978-1-8448-6648-9

2 4 6 8 10 9 7 5 3 1

Art Editor Louise Turpin. Typeset in Cera PRO
Map illustration © OpenStreetMap contributors, created with Datawrapper
Printed and bound in India by Replika Press Pvt. Ltd.

To find out more about our authors and books visit www.bloomsbury.com
and sign up for our newsletters

THE WALKER'S GUIDE TO THE Castles OF Britain

60 Inspiring Walks through Time

Julia Goodfellow-Smith

C✛NWAY
LONDON · OXFORD · NEW YORK · NEW DELHI · SYDNEY

CONTENTS

Castles map ... 6
Introduction ... 7

1 ALNWICK CASTLE ... 16

2 ARUNDEL CASTLE ... 20

3 BALMORAL CASTLE ... 24

4 BAMBURGH CASTLE ... 28

5 BLAIR CASTLE ... 32

6 CAERLAVEROCK CASTLE ... 36

7 CARDONESS CASTLE ... 40

8 CARISBROOKE CASTLE ... 44

9 CARLISLE CASTLE ... 48

10 CASTELL BIWMARES / *BEAUMARIS CASTLE* ... 52

11 CASTELL CAERDYDD / *CARDIFF CASTLE* ... 56

12 CASTELL CAERFFILI / *CAERPHILLY CASTLE* ... 60

13 CASTELL CAERNARFON ... 64

14 CASTELL CARREG CENNEN ... 68

15 CASTELL CAS-GWENT / *CHEPSTOW CASTLE* ... 72

16 CASTELL COCH ... 76

17 CASTELL CONWY ... 80

18 CASTELL CYDWELI / *KIDWELLY CASTLE* ... 84

19 CASTELL DINAS BRÂN ... 88

20 CASTELL DINEFWR ... 92

21 CASTELL HARLECH ... 96

22 CASTELL LLANSTEFFAN ... 100

23 CASTELL POWIS ... 104

24 CASTELL Y WAUN / *CHIRK CASTLE* ... 108

25 CASTLE CAMPBELL ... 112

26 CASTLE STALKER ... 116

ABOVE Castell Caernarfon.

ABOVE Gylen Castle.

27 CLIFFORD'S TOWER	120
28 CORFE CASTLE	124
29 DARTMOUTH CASTLE	128
30 DOUNE CASTLE	132
31 DOVER CASTLE	136
32 DUMBARTON CASTLE	140
33 DUNNOTTAR CASTLE	144
34 DUNSTAFFNAGE & DUNOLLIE CASTLES	148
35 DURHAM CASTLE	152
36 EDINBURGH CASTLE	156
37 EILEAN DONAN CASTLE	160
38 FARLEIGH HUNGERFORD CASTLE	164
39 FRAMLINGHAM CASTLE	168
40 GLAMIS CASTLE	172
41 GOODRICH CASTLE	176
42 GYLEN CASTLE	180
43 INVERARAY CASTLE	184
44 KENILWORTH CASTLE	188
45 KILCHURN CASTLE	192
46 LANCASTER CASTLE	196
47 LEEDS CASTLE	200
48 LINCOLN CASTLE	204
49 MANORBIER CASTLE	208
50 NORWICH CASTLE	212
51 ORFORD CASTLE	216
52 PENDENNIS CASTLE	220
53 SCARBOROUGH CASTLE	224
54 ST MICHAEL'S MOUNT	228
55 STIRLING CASTLE	232
56 THREAVE CASTLE	236
57 TINTAGEL CASTLE	240
58 TOWER OF LONDON	244
59 URQUHART CASTLE	248
60 WINDSOR CASTLE	252

Acknowledgements 256

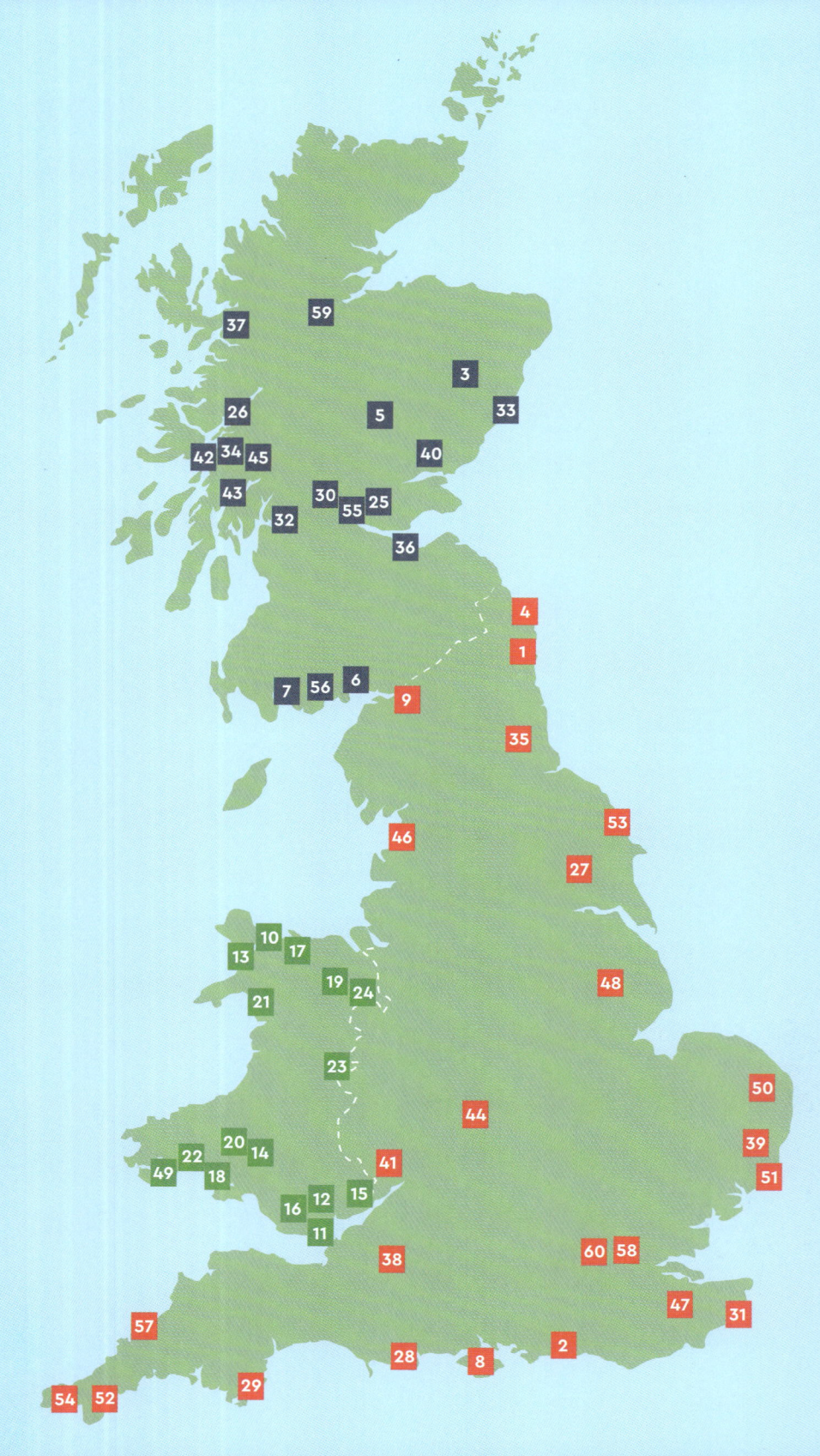

INTRODUCTION

The earliest dominant fortifications in the British landscape are mainly Iron Age hill forts, the earthen ringworks around hilltops. In their prime, timber palisades crowned the top of steep-sided ditches, creating a strong defence against neighbouring tribes.

The next wave of fortifications was built by the Romans to support their invasion. Their forts and fortresses (distinguished by size) were initially made from turf and timber, and some reused hill fort sites. Many were rebuilt in stone when time and resources allowed.

BELOW Castell Conwy.

ABOVE The Tower of London.

When the Romans left, the local tribes that remained continued to occupy many of the same places. Later, when powerful people or invaders wanted to build a castle, the remains of a Roman fortification were sometimes reused, creating layers of history on one site.

Castles were usually built as a demonstration of wealth and power, to defend against invaders, and as a base from which to mount raids and invasions. Buildings that appear dark and foreboding now were often rendered and painted in a light colour, making them more conspicuous.

In England, most of the castles we see today were built after the Norman Conquest of 1066. As the Normans had found it so easy to invade England across the Channel, they raised a series of fortifications around the south coast to protect it from another invasion. In London, they built a massive tower in the city as a sign of their sovereignty (the Tower of London) and a ring of smaller towers around the city, of which Windsor is one. Even once the conquest was officially over and England was in Norman hands, powerful men rebelled against their overlords. This resulted in the construction of more castles across the country by both sides.

Over the centuries, power struggles continued, and castles were besieged, demolished and built as required. As the relationship with Europe waxed and waned, castles and additional fortifications were constructed in response to the perceived threat of invasion.

Further west, castles were built by the princes of Wales to assert their authority over the surrounding lands. The princes jostled for power with each other and the Normans to the east. The Normans placed a series of powerful Marcher lords along the Welsh borders, whose allegiance was not necessarily guaranteed. This resulted in the border between England and Wales moving east and west along with the power base, marked by a proliferation of castles.

In the south of Wales, the Normans pushed west, building castles as they progressed. These protected the Anglo-Norman settlers and gave them a base from which they could drive north across the country.

Various wars ensued, and Wales was finally conquered in 1283, some 200 years after England capitulated. Rebels continued to plague the crown, so Edward I built a ring of castles around Snowconia in an attempt to keep those rebels under control. These are known as the Ring of Iron. Many of those castles were supplied from the sea to avoid potential delay or defeat in the Welsh mountain passes.

In Scotland, many castles are tower houses built by clans to protect them from neighbouring clans. Once Edward I had conquered Wales, he turned his attention to Scotland, and the border was hotly contested for many centuries, resulting in a series of castles that now stand in each country.

As relatively peaceful times ensued, many castles were enlarged and beautified, becoming grand homes, some with elaborate landscaping and formal gardens. There was, of course, more conflict after this, including the British Civil Wars of 1642–51 (often called the English Civil War). During

BELOW Dunstaffnage Castle.

this period, many castles were destroyed, either under bombardment or to stop them from being used again (known as 'slighting').

Since then, castles have been brought back into service as required. During the two world wars, many were used for gun emplacements, and some for other specialist purposes.

Hopefully, the castles of Britain will never need to be used in conflict again.

Castles were usually seats of power as well as strongholds. Many were used to collect taxes, house courts and imprison people. Indeed, Lincoln Castle still houses a Crown Court, and it was only earlier this century that the prison in Lancaster Castle was closed.

LOOK OUT FOR

You will often see or hear reference to the motte and bailey. The motte is not the moat. In fact, it is quite the opposite; the motte is the mound upon which the Normans built their dominant tower, known as a keep. The keep was usually the building in which the lord and his family either lived or could retreat into at times of siege. However, castles also needed space for all the fighting forces and services that supported the family. These were usually housed in an enclosure, initially surrounded by a timber palisade and later a stone wall. This enclosure is known as the bailey. The stone walls are known as curtain walls and are strengthened with additional towers. The towers enabled defenders to shoot attackers as they tried to surmount or undermine the wall.

The main entrance to a castle is usually the most heavily defended point. Many castles are either on a promontory or have a ditch dug around them. When the ditch is filled with water, it is known as a moat. These days, moats are often attractive bodies of water, but in the past they would have been full of sewage and other disgusting substances, partly as a means of disposing of this waste and partly as a deterrent to interlopers.

Entry to the castle was often by a drawbridge over the moat. The drawbridge was lifted to make entry difficult. If the castle was caught unawares, and the drawbridge was still down when the troops arrived, there were additional lines of defence. Archers could shoot them through arrow slits, defenders could pour boiling water and oil through murder holes or drop stones on to them. Metal grids known as portcullises and wooden doors would further complicate entry.

RIGHT Beaumaris Castle (credit: Crown copyright (2023) Cymru Wales).

COUNTRYSIDE CODE AND SCOTTISH OUTDOOR ACCESS CODE

The Countryside Code applies in England and Wales, and the Outdoor Access Code applies in Scotland. They are both based on similar principles – that walkers should:

- Respect everyone, including other path users and landowners. Park responsibly. Leave gates as they find them. Keep dogs under control and remove their waste. Keep to the path (England and Wales only – Scotland has open access for walkers).
- Protect the environment. Don't disturb wildlife. Leave no trace – take litter home.
- Take responsibility for their own actions. Behave safely.
- Enjoy the outdoors. Have fun!

The author has completed all these walks, which were accessible and enjoyable at the time of writing. However, paths can be closed or diverted, or become overgrown in summer, and the landmarks used to describe the routes can be changed. If you notice any issues, please contact us at adlardcoles@bloomsbury.com so we can make amendments in future editions. Castle opening hours are also subject to change – please check before visiting.

THE WALKS

Many castles stand in spectacular or beautiful landscapes, surrounded by excellent walking country. The castles in this book have been chosen for enjoyment of the buildings, alongside a fabulous walk in the surrounding area.

The walks should take around two to three hours to complete, so you can visit the castle and experience the landscape in which it sits in one day. All either start and end at the castle or pass it en route.

The maps indicate the route of the walk. We recommend downloading the GPX file to use with an app on your phone to aid navigation. GPX files are compatible with commonly used apps, such as Google Maps. The GPX files can be downloaded from bloomsbury.com/castle-maps. None of the walks require specialist knowledge. Most are low level and

on good paths. However, shoes with good grip are usually helpful, and we always recommend a set of waterproofs.

Most walks are accessible for people with dogs, although two pass across land where dogs are not permitted, and some have stiles. The walk description gives guidance about surfaces and likely challenges.
It is a good idea to carry a small first-aid kit with you, as well as water and snacks.

INSECTS

Ticks are becoming more prevalent in Britain. Their bites do not hurt, but they can transmit nasty diseases. You can reduce the risk of bites by wearing long sleeves and trousers and using insect repellent. Check for ticks after walks, particularly during the warmer months when you have brushed against vegetation. If you find one, remove the tick carefully as quickly as possible. If you develop a rash, bull's-eye ring around the bite or flu-like symptoms after being bitten, please talk to your GP.

Midges and other flying insects can be a nuisance, particularly on warm days in damp areas. While you're walking, you're not usually a target. While stationary, the best way to avoid being bitten is to cover up and apply insect repellent on exposed skin.

ENTRY FEES

Some castles in this book are free to enter. However, many are not. If you are planning to visit several, it is worth considering membership of English Heritage, Cadw or Historic Scotland. All have reciprocal arrangements in place. The National Trust and the National Trust for Scotland also have reciprocal arrangements for members.

BELOW LEFT Dinas Bran, BELOW RIGHT Threave Castle, OVERLEAF Caerlaverock Castle.

ALNWICK CASTLE

A castle was first built in Alnwick by the Normans shortly after they conquered England to assert their position in the Scottish borderlands. Since then, bits have been demolished and added, so what we see today is an amalgam of styles through the ages. The Norman keep is now a sumptuous Italianate palace – far removed from its original state.

The castle has impressive fortifications, including a creative assortment of death-traps in the barbican, ready to foil intruders. This includes pits full of spikes with trapdoors above that would be released when men were on top of them, murder holes, and an unusual dummy spiral stair that leads up to nowhere. Those who ran to the top could be speared through carefully placed openings.

The castle was not robust enough to cope with cannon fire; once cannons were introduced into warfare, its role switched from fortification to administrative centre for the Duke of Northumberland's estates. The duke's family has owned the castle for most of the last 700 years, and it remains their family home during the winter.

You may be familiar with the castle as a setting for Harry Potter (remember his first broomstick flying lesson?) and Christmas specials of *Downton Abbey*.

WALK DETAILS

START/FINISH
Hulne Park gates, Alnwick NE66 3HX

DISTANCE
10.5km (6½ miles)

PARKING
On road near start, castle or town car parks

PUBLIC TRANSPORT
Bus from Alnmouth station to Alnwick Canongate

REFRESHMENTS
Pubs and cafés in Alnwick, café in castle

TOILETS
At castle and The Shambles and Greenwell Road, Alnwick

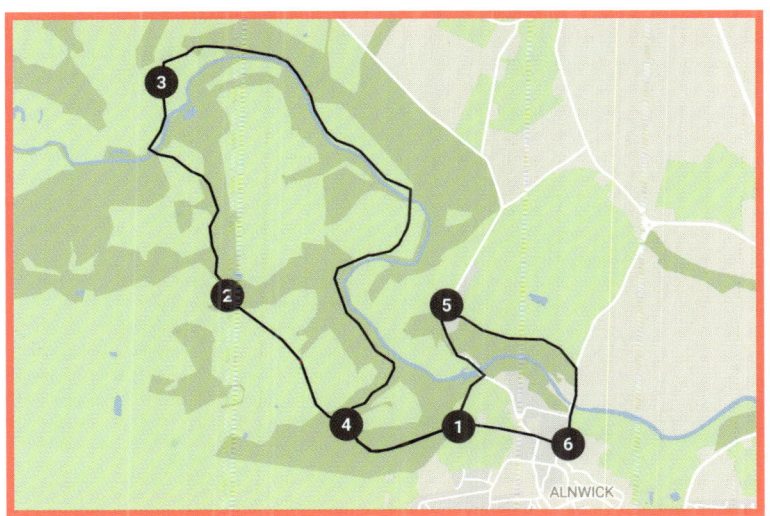

THE WALK

An easy walk through parkland and woodland, over rolling hills and alongside rivers, mostly through Hulne Park. The park is open daily from 11am to 4pm and is occasionally closed for private events
Please check before setting off:
https://northumberlandestates.co.uk/the-estate/walks-trails/
Dogs are not allowed. The second loop provides the best view of the castle.

1 Head west through the gates into Hulne Park and along the drive.
You will be following the red waymarkers along the route.

> Hulne Park is one of three parks that once belonged to the castle. They were primarily designed to provide timber for maintaining the castle, and Hulne Park still performs this function today. They were also stocked with deer for hunting, and continue to fulfil this purpose, too. The 4,500 hectares of land were enclosed by a wall 21km (13 miles) long.
>
> The park is one of the last remaining homes of the red squirrel in England. Grey squirrels were introduced into Britain by the Victorians as game. Since then they have been spreading and the reds have been retreating. Red squirrels are elusive, but if you keep your eyes peeled, you might be lucky enough to see one.

Cross a stone bridge. At the first junction, bear right past Old Moor Lodge. At the next junction, stay left. After some time, you reach the drive to Park Farm.

2 Turn right here, then take the first left, following the red waymarkers.
Eventually, this track reaches a bridge over the river. Cross and then turn right onto another track. You can see the remains of Hulne Priory ahead. Take the grassy path up to the left edge of the ruins.

> The priory was founded by Carmelite friars who were

LEFT Alnwick castle from Lion Bridge.

ABOVE The river and parkland from Lion Bridge.

granted grazing and specific foraging rights within the park. By the mid-18th century, it was in ruins. When the first Duke and Duchess Percy decided to make the castle their home, the ruins became a place for them to entertain guests on carriage rides, and the duchess planted a garden here. On her death, the duke built the picnic house as a memorial to her, along with Brizlee Tower, which you can see on the neighbouring hill.

3 **After exploring the ruins, exit through the gate and turn right along the cinder track, following it around to the right.**

Through the gate, turn right downhill. When you reach the river, continue in the same direction on the track with the river on your right for about 1.2km (¾ mile), then cross the bridge. Continue ahead through the parkland and into trees on the far side. Stay left at the next junction of tracks. The river is still to your left. At the next junction, turn right.

This track brings you back to Old Moor Lodge that you passed earlier.

4 **Continue ahead and retrace your steps to the entrance of the park.** The first loop of the walk is complete.

For the second loop, turn left onto the public footpath just outside the park gates, down through a meadow to a corner of the estate wall, and then alongside it until you reach a road.

Turn left over the bridge and follow the road for about 500m (⅓ mile).

5 **A few metres after the end of the stone wall on the right, turn right up what looks like a private drive,** but has a public footpath running along it. Follow the drive around to the left, and you will see the path ahead. Follow this path until you reach a road. Turn right along the road.

> The bridge at the bottom is Lion Bridge. In the 19th century, the park was relandscaped by 'Capability' Brown. Trees were planted to obscure sight of the castle until this point, so that visitors had the best possible view from the bridge.

ALNWICK CASTLE

Cross the bridge and continue ahead to reach the castle entrance.

6 From here, turn right down Bailiffgate to return to the start.

TOP Alnwick Castle barbican and gatehouse.

ABOVE The ruins of Hulne Priory.

ALNWICK CASTLE

2 ARUNDEL CASTLE

A figure-of-eight shape, similar in design to Windsor, Arundel Castle dominates both the landscape and the town. The castle wall forms the western boundary of the ancient town centre, and from the east it stands proud on a hill above the flat river valley.

Shortly after the Normans invaded, the castle was built as one of a chain along the south coast to deter anyone else thinking of following their lead. Initially, the keep and defences were made from timber. These were replaced with stone – mainly local flint – over the following century. The keep, however, was built using stone from Caen in Normandy – a significant status symbol at the time.

The castle continued to be built and rebuilt over the centuries. Much of the original Norman stonework is still visible, along with significant Victorian renovations. The modern gardens are almost as impressive as the castle itself.

The castle was not impervious to attack. Indeed, it changed hands three times during the British Civil Wars. The final siege only lasted 18 days, as the attackers knew that Swanbourne Lake was the source of the castle's water – and drained it. Severely dehydrated, the defending troops had no choice but to surrender.

WALK DETAILS

START/FINISH
Mill Road car park, Arundel BN18 9PA

DISTANCE
17.25km (10¾ miles)

PARKING
At start and Points 2 & 4

PUBLIC TRANSPORT
Train to Arundel, bus to Arundel Riverbank

REFRESHMENTS
Pubs and cafés in Arundel, café at castle and at Swanbourne Lake

TOILETS
At start and castle

BELOW Arundel Castle from the riverbank.

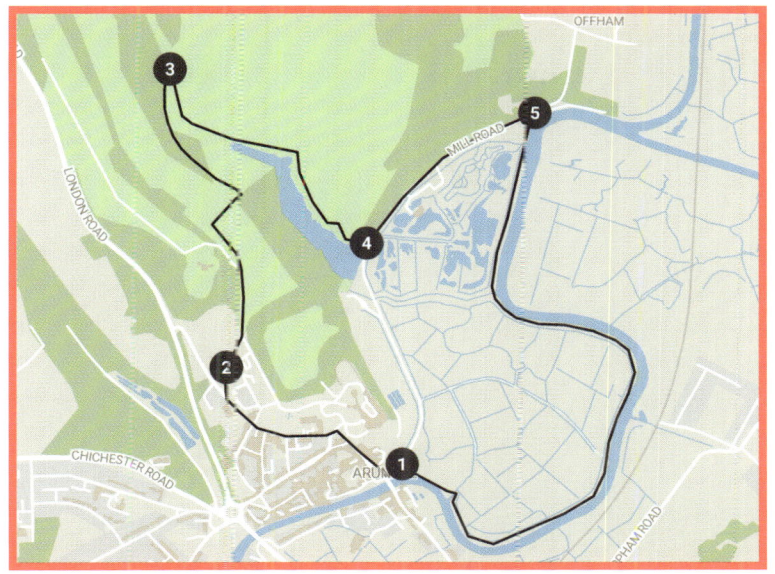

THE WALK

An easy walk around a gap in the South Downs. The first leg is through the historic town, then the sweeping landscapes of Arundel Park, past the Hiorne Tower and along Swanbourne Lake. After a stretch on a quiet road, the route returns along the River Arun with fantastic views of the castle.

1 From the car park, turn left onto Mill Road, then right onto High Street, through the centre of the old town. Where the road turns to the left, continue with the castle walls on your right. Pass the Catholic cathedral, and follow the wall bearing right away from the road.

Before reaching the cathedral, you pass the flint and stone church of St Nicholas, which was built at the end of the 14th century. It is the Protestant parish church of Arundel, although, thanks to a quirk of history, part of the church (the Fitzalan Chapel) is Catholic.

BELOW Castle Park (photo courtesy of Arundel Estate).

ARUNDEL CASTLE

This chapel is the mausoleum of the Dukes of Norfolk. This area is separated from the rest of the church by a screen and can only be accessed from within the castle grounds. In the main body of the church, look out for the stone font, which might pre-date the church, the medieval stone pulpit and the now faint paintings on the walls of the north aisle.

The cathedral was designed by Joseph Aloysius Hansom, who is best known for inventing the hansom cab. It was built by Duke Henry as nothing more than the Catholic parish church in 1869, and became a cathedral almost 100 years later on the creation of the diocese of Arundel and Brighton.

Cross a drive and take the path ahead into Arundel Park.

2 When through the gates, continue to follow the drive (public footpath). Turn right at the waymarker between the solitary oak tree and Hiorne Tower.

Hiorne Tower is named after its architect, Francis Hiorne. It is a triangular folly, built in 1787, and now Grade II listed.

ABOVE Hiorne Tower.

At the edge of the woods, follow the waymarker down some steps and then left along a track. This track gradually drops into a valley.

3 Turn right down the valley, and then stay on the track along the length of Swanbourne Lake to a road.

The water level of Swanbourne Lake dropped so far in 1989 that the remains of a WWII German bomber were visible after nearly half a century of being underwater. It is thought that the plane was shot down while heading to bomb the British airbase at Farnborough. Along with the plane, an unexploded bomb was exposed. Imagine the spectacle if that had exploded underwater.

In the summer, look out for swifts, swallows, house martins and sand martins here. All are migrants, their arrival signalling the start of summer. Swifts spend all their life on the wing, except when they are nesting, and screech as they wheel around overhead. Swallows can be identified by their long forked tail and white chest. Martins have short forked tails.

4 Turn left onto the road for about 1km (⅔ mile), past the Wildfowl and Wetlands Trust centre to a hamlet by the river.

The wetland centre provides a habitat for many wild birds, and also has some you might not expect to see. For example, Pelican Cove is home to Dalmatian pelicans, which were once common in the UK. As people ate them and drained wetlands to create farmland, life for pelicans in the UK became very difficult. They are now locally extinct in the wild and vulnerable to extinction in other parts of the world.

5 When entering the hamlet, turn right through the Black Rabbit pub car park onto a path, with the river on your left. After crossing a stream with sluice gates, look right for spectacular views of the castle. Further along, the cathedral also comes into sight on the right. This path eventually leads back to Mill Road car park and High Street.

BELOW Arundel Cathedral and Castle from the riverbank.

3 BALMORAL CASTLE

The first house was built at Balmoral in 1390. By the early 1500s, it had been transformed into a tower. A hundred years later, it had expanded to include turrets and a walled enclosure with courtyards.

In 1848, Queen Victoria and Prince Albert leased the castle sight unseen. The area reminded them of Albert's homeland, and they fell in love with the place. Four years later, they bought it. The following year, they laid the foundation stone for a new castle. All that remains of the old castle is a stone in the garden that marks the position of the original front door.

To celebrate the purchase, the family and their household processed up one of the hills on the estate and built a cairn to the sound of bagpipes. Everyone present laid a stone, and Albert climbed to the top to place the last one. The cairn took just an hour to build and has stood for over 170 years.

This was the first cairn of many to be erected on the estate, with the jewel in the crown being a pyramid raised in memory of Prince Albert himself. Balmoral Castle remains the royal family's Scottish home.

WALK DETAILS

START/FINISH
Balmoral car park, Crathie AB35 5TL

DISTANCE
9.25km (5¾ miles)

PARKING
At start

PUBLIC TRANSPORT
Bus from Ballater to Balmoral Road End, Crathie

REFRESHMENTS
Café in castle

TOILETS
At start

THE WALK
Find out why Queen Victoria fell in love with this area as you explore the Balmoral Estate, visiting the celebratory cairns and the pyramid commemorating Prince Albert's life. Mainly woodland paths through

conifer plantations, some steep climbs. Fabulous views over the surrounding valleys and the castle itself.

1 From the main road, take the lane next to the circular building housing the post office and toilets. At the T-junction, turn right. This lane crosses the River Dee.

2 On the far side of the bridge, turn right onto the B-road, then left towards Royal Lochnagar Distillery. At the first bend to the left, turn right over a small stone bridge and through the gate into the Balmoral Estate and Easter Balmoral village.

LEFT Balmoral Castle from the hills above.

BELOW Prince Albert's cairn.

BALMORAL CASTLE

Turn left, following a sign for the cairn walks. Opposite the gates to a grand house on the right, turn left, signposted Prince Albert's cairn.

ABOVE The River Dee as it passes close to the castle.

RIGHT The path to a celebratory cairn.

> *The first cairn you come to is dedicated to Princess Beatrice, married to HRH Prince Henry Maurice of Battenberg on 23 July 1885. This is one of a series of cairns built to commemorate the marriages of Queen Victoria's children.*

3 At the top of a steep climb, you will reach the cairn to Prince Albert.

> *This cairn is made from dressed stone and is far larger than the others. The pyramid is 42 feet (3.9 metres) square, each square foot representing one year of Prince Albert's life.*

4 From the cairn, continue along the clear path down to a track. Turn right. At the next junction, turn left through a high gate. When a building comes into view on the left, look to the right for a footpath that starts to run parallel to the track. Note: the junction is before the gate for the building, and the path is significantly smaller than the previous cairns path. After a few hundred metres, look for the turn to the right, which is signposted cairn walks, and head uphill here. After a short sharp rise, you'll reach the cairn celebrating the marriage of Princess Alice of England and Prince Louis of Hesse Darmstadt on 1 July 1862.

5 Continue along the path, and in a while you will come to a T-junction of paths. Turn right uphill. At the next junction, turn left. After about 200m (220yds), turn onto a narrow path off to the left, to visit another cairn.

> *This one commemorates the marriage of Prince Arthur Duke of Connaught and Strathearn to Princess Louise Margaret of Prussia on 13 March 1879.*

6 Continue past the cairn to return via a different route to the main path. Turn left. As this path heads downhill, look for a side path on the left that leads to another cairn.

> *The cairn celebrates the wedding of Prince Leopold Duke of Albany who married Princess Helen of Waldeck on 27 April 1882. From here, there are fine views over Balmoral Castle.*

7 Retrace your steps back to the main path and turn left downhill. At the next junction of paths, turn right.

Look out for the statue of John Brown on your right, one of Queen Victoria's servants.

At the next junction, turn right signposted car park. Stay right at the following junction and after that turn left, following car park signs. This path leads to a gravel track. Turn left downhill. After a while, you will recognise this drive from the outgoing walk. When you reach the gates of the estate, head through them and back down the tarmac lane.

At the bottom of the hill, turn left and follow this road to the castle entrance.

On the right, you will pass a curling lodge. In the winter, the stream can be blocked here to flood the field in front of the building and create a curling rink.

To finish the walk, cross the bridge back to the car park.

BALMORAL CASTLE

4 BAMBURGH CASTLE

Bamburgh Castle is best known for its stunning setting on the wild Northumberland coast and its leading role in *The Last Kingdom* television series.

Bamburgh was already populated before the Romans arrived in AD 43. In AD 547, the first Anglo-Saxon king of Northumberland built a wooden fortress here, which was replaced by a stone one after 60 years. When the Normans arrived almost 500 years later, they used the castle as a base to attack Scotland. In 1603, Scotland and England united under one monarch. The castle was no longer needed for military purposes and became privately owned.

This is where the castle's history diverges from many others, as it became a hub of philanthropy. In 1721, the owner's will set up a trust to maintain the castle and a charity to help the poor and sick of the village. This led to the establishment of a hospital, school – and the world's first coastguard station. During foggy weather, a signal cannon was fired towards the village to alert the villagers. They set up watches and beach patrols, helped shipwreck survivors, provided burials to those who didn't survive, and built the first lifeboat to save those in the water.

THE WALK

A beautiful beach walk with views over the Farne Islands and of the castle from both east and west. Inland, the route passes through farmland and along a road to complete the circuit. The walk can easily be split into two loops and does not require specialist footwear.

WALK DETAILS

START/FINISH
Castle entrance, Bamburgh NE69 7DF

DISTANCE
10km (6¼ miles)

PARKING
Castle or Links Road car park at start. Car park along beach road between Points 4 & 5

PUBLIC TRANSPORT
Bus from Newcastle or Berwick-Upon-Tweed to Bamburgh Lord Crewe Hotel

REFRESHMENTS
On the B1342 in Bamburgh and in castle

TOILETS
On the B1342 in Bamburgh and in castle

LEFT Bamburgh Castle from the southeast.

1 From the castle car park, take the gate in the far corner onto the sand dunes and turn immediately right onto the England Coast Path. The sea is on your left beyond the dunes.

> *The Bowl Hole is to your left. This is where an archaeological dig in the early 21st century unearthed 110 Anglo-Saxon skeletons.*

After meeting the road, the path turns towards the dunes. Where it turns right, continue ahead towards the sea. Where the path forks, head left towards the gate. Look behind you for a view of the castle. Continue through the gate and the dunes to the shore.

> *The islands you see directly ahead of you are the Farne Islands.*

Turn right and continue ahead for about 700m (½ mile) to the next rocky outcrop.

2 Turn right on a path that leads directly away from the sea just before the pillbox on the dune. This will lead you to a road. Cross and continue ahead on a farm track. Look right for more views of the castle.

Follow the track as it continues through the farm and then kinks right to continue on the right-hand side of a hedge. At the end of the field, the track turns right and heads directly towards the castle.

When you reach some houses, head around the right-hand side of the wall, and continue towards the castle over a series of drives. The next stretch takes you along the edge of a pasture, then across to a road.

3 Turn left. Follow the road past the castle and out past the town. Where the pavement runs out, a narrow path runs along the verge. After about 1km (⅔ mile), the narrow path bends away from the road and meets a footpath that turns right to Budle Point.

4 Follow the waymarkers across the golf course.

> *Holy Island and Lindisfarne Castle are visible across the water ahead. In AD 635, King Oswald of Northumbria invited a monk from Iona to be his bishop and granted him the tidal island of Lindisfarne on which to build a monastery. In the 670s, Cuthbert joined the monastery and ultimately*

BAMBURGH CASTLE

became the bishop. Eleven years after he died, the monks opened his tomb to find his body intact. Consequently, he was sainted and his shrine (now in Durham Cathedral) became a major pilgrimage centre.

Leave the golf course through a small gate and continue downhill towards a couple of buildings. Skirt to the left of the buildings and continue in the general direction of Lindisfarne.

When you reach the tarmac path, turn right. Follow signs for the coast path, rising gently. The path leads back onto the golf course. Follow the blue waymarkers downhill. Turn right at the bottom, past a pillbox. Continue along this path between the golf course and the sea.

It is not long before the castle comes into view, completely dominating the landscape. Out to sea on its left are the Farne Islands, two of which house lighthouses and one a chapel.

The path is well waymarked until you reach the golf clubhouse. Walk in front of the clubhouse and then between a row of cottages and the sea along a tarmac lane. This lane will take you almost all the way back to the castle. Alternatively, walk along the beach.

When you reach some houses, look for the England Coast Path sign.

ABOVE The England Coast Path through the dunes.

5 **Bear left along the track towards the castle**. At the cricket pitch, continue ahead to the far side of the castle, where the route ends.

ABOVE Looking southeast along the beach.

BELOW Bamburgh Castle at sunset.

BLAIR CASTLE

The Stewarts and Murrays (one family) have lived at Blair Castle for over 700 years. The original castle was a complex tower house built in 1269. Over the centuries, it has been extended several times into the impressive home you see today.

Shortly after the British Civil Wars, the castle was captured by Cromwell's army, as the family remained Royalists. This did not stop the earl from making a good marriage – to Lady Amelia Stanley, heiress to the Isle of Man. When the British monarchy resumed in 1660, the castle was returned to the Murrays. The family siphoned off revenue from the Isle of Man to extend the castle. Consequently, the island suffered from a lack of investment, leading to a booming smuggling economy, which the British government disapproved of. The family was ultimately forced to sell the island's sovereignty to the British government to resolve the situation.

BELOW Blair Castle.

WALK DETAILS

START/FINISH
Blair Atholl railway station, PH18 5SL

DISTANCE
10.75km (6¾ miles)

PARKING
In village or Glen Tilt car park between Points 2 & 3

PUBLIC TRANSPORT
Train to Blair Atholl

REFRESHMENTS
In village and castle

TOILETS
In village car park, in castle

In 1844, Queen Victoria stayed at the castle and was so impressed with the men who guarded her that she granted the duke and his men

the right to bear arms. The Atholl Highlanders is the only private army in Europe and guards the duke.

THE WALK
Walk in the steps of the condemned and those who chose to view the public hangings on Tom na Croiche hill, explore the forestry tracks of the Atholl Estates, watch streams cascade down gorges and cross a meadow buzzing with life, with a view of the castle in its landscape.

1 From the station, head towards the Atholl Arms Hotel. Turn right to cross in front of the hotel and continue through the village until you reach the entrance into the castle grounds. Turn left through the gates and up the avenue of lime trees to the far end of the campsite on the right.
NOTE: if you are arriving outside castle opening hours, these gates might be closed. If so, turn left from the station instead of right, take the first track on your right, and then the next right. This route will take you to the avenue of limes at Point 2.

ABOVE Balvenie Pillar.

BLAIR CASTLE

2 Turn right along the track (or straight over if you were unable to walk through the main gates). Follow this track past the woodland lodges and into the forest to the Glen Tilt car park. Turn left in front of the cottage. Where the road forks, take some steps up on the right, signposted Balvenie Pillar. At the top of the steep slope, you will come to the obelisk.

This was erected in 1755 as a reminder of the last public hanging that took place here, more than a century earlier.

3 Continue along the path across the top of the hill, over a bridge to the neighbouring rise, and then down to a track. Turn left. This is Glen Tilt. You can hear the river in the gorge to your right.

Keep an eye out for red squirrels as you walk.

After about 1.5km (1 mile), fork left up a narrower track that rises up through mainly birch woodland. The track crosses a small gorge with a fierce stream running down it, and then enters coniferous forest. On reaching a T-junction with another track, turn left flat along the hill. After 500m (⅓ mile), take the track that forks to the right through a gate in a deer fence until you reach a reservoir on the left.

4 Continue ahead along the flat. Where this track turns to the right, go through another gate in a deer fence. Cross the meadow ahead with wide open views to the left and in front. Pass through another gate into more forestry. At a crossroads of tracks, continue ahead. This track soon joins another, heading in the same direction. Cross a small stone bridge, and then fork to the left. The valley is now dropping steeply to your left and this track drops more gently to a bridge. Cross the river and gorge here. Turn left, and after a couple of hundred metres, turn right along a track, signposted The Whim viewpoint.

From the Whim monument, there are fabulous views along the valley and over the castle turret.

5 Return to the track that runs along the top of the gorge and turn right. Pass some sheds on your right and stay left, keeping the gorge on your left and the houses on your right. Eventually, this track reaches a tarmac lane along an estate wall. Turn right along the lane. At the end of the estate wall, turn left down the tarmac drive.

BELOW The view from the meadow (Point 4).

BLAIR CASTLE

To your left is Diana's Grove, a woodland of exotic trees (entry fees apply).

This drive leads to the castle.

6 Walk in front of the building and turn left over a footbridge and over the stream. Turn right down the tarmac drive, which joins the avenue of limes. Take the first track on the right, between a meadow and a woodland. When you reach a tarmac lane, turn left. At the next junction, turn left to return to the station.

ABOVE The reservoir between Points 3 and 4.
BELOW Blair Castle (credit: Alex Baxter).

CAERLAVEROCK CASTLE

Caerlaverock Castle is Britain's only triangular castle and the only one in Scotland with a moat. It is now inland but was initially built to defend the coast against English incursions. The castle enclosure, which housed essential services such as smithies and brewhouses, stretched from the port near the old castle to where the visitor centre stands today.

The castle was besieged in the Wars of Independence with England, and although the ensuing victory was not significant, it was well documented. The king's army had 87 knights and 3,000 men, and the castle had 60. It must have been clear that they didn't stand a chance against such a large army, and they surrendered after just two days.

The castle continued to be a party to the conflict between England and Scotland. When the countries were unified in 1603, the Maxwells built a mansion inside the castle and put windows into the curtain wall in anticipation of peace.

This was a bit premature, and the castle was besieged again during the British Civil Wars. This time, the garrison held for 13 weeks before surrendering. That was the death knell of the castle, as it was partially dismantled so it could not be used again.

WALK DETAILS

START/FINISH
Caerlaverock NNR car park, Dumfries DG1 4RU

DISTANCE
8.5km (5¼ miles)

PARKING
At start or at castle

PUBLIC TRANSPORT
Bus from Dumfries to Caerlaverock Castle

REFRESHMENTS
Café at castle

TOILETS
At castle

RIGHT The boardwalk across the marsh.
BELOW Caerlaverock Castle.

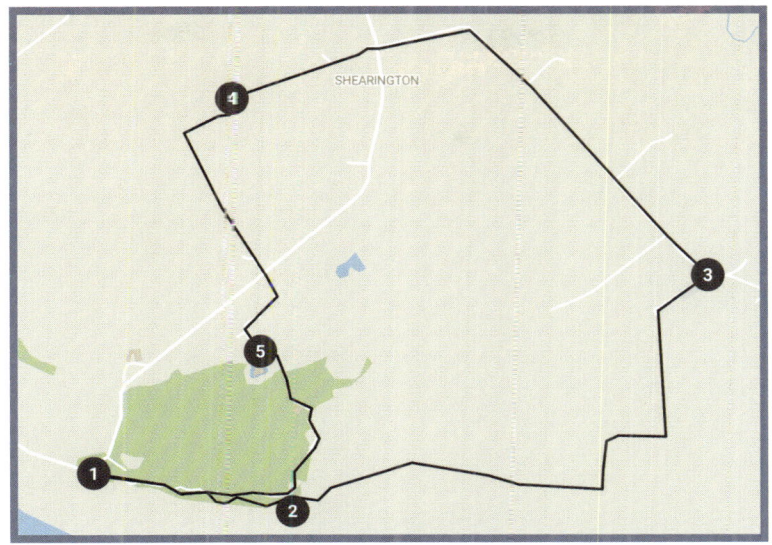

THE WALK

A flat walk around the salt marshes of this National Nature Reserve on the Solway Firth, with one climb to an Iron Age hill fort that offers fantastic views across the water to the surrounding hills. Take your binoculars – this is a haven for wildlife, particularly overwintering birds.

1 Take the path into the nature reserve with the bay on your right. At the junction of paths, take the right fork. This heads along the edge of the salt marsh.

The scenery here changes dramatically as the tides rise and cover much of the marshes, then fall leaving them exposed.

CAERLAVEROCK CASTLE

> *The mudbanks are full of little critters that provide food for the 140,000 birds that arrive here for the winter months.*
>
> *In summer, the marsh is grazed by cattle to keep the vegetation short, which improves the habitat for geese and toads – this nature reserve provides a home to the natterjack toad, which is Scotland's rarest amphibian.*

At the edge of the woods, you will reach a junction near a bird hide.

2 Continue ahead along the boardwalk on the edge of the salt marsh. After a little over 1km (⅔ mile), turn left onto a boardwalk heading inland. After a short distance, follow it to the right. At the end of this section of boardwalk, turn left onto the track, heading inland. At the farm, turn right down the drive to the road.

3 Turn left and follow the road.

> *After a couple of fields, look left for your first view of the castle.*

At the T-junction after about 1.5km (1 mile), cross the road and head straight up the hill opposite. Where the track bends to the right, continue straight up the hill through the woodland then the field to the stand of trees at the top of the hill.

4 Pass through the gate, then turn left.

> *You are now on Ward Law, an old hill fort and the site of a Roman army camp. Some of the hill fort ramparts are visible, but there is nothing to see of the army camp at ground level. From here, there are fantastic views across the Solway Firth and to the castle.*

Follow the path through the woods, and then as it drops down some steps, between fields and left towards the castle. Continue ahead until you reach the road. Cross the road and follow the lane to the castle.

5 Follow the drive around to the left of the castle. This leads to the remains of the old castle.

> *The first fortification we are aware of on this site dates back to AD 950. It would have been built for the Lords of Nithsdale. Although it is now 800m (½ mile) away, it was built close to the shore of the Solway Firth and had a harbour a little to the south. It started life as a timber*

CAERLAVEROCK CASTLE

LEFT Ward Law hill fort.
ABOVE The view from Ward Law.

structure, surrounded by moats and with a defended outer bailey to one side.

Around 1220, Alexander II granted the land and titles to the Maxwells. At that time, the land was a part of Scotland and Maxwell built a castle to defend against the English. After 50 years, his nephew inherited and decided to build a new castle 200m (220yds) away, which is the 'new' castle we see today. The layout of the old castle can be seen in the woods, along with the moat.

Continue on the track through Castle Wood. At the cottage, the track becomes a path. Continue along this path through the woods, ignoring side paths, back to the start.

These are ancient woodlands that were once coppiced to provide fuel and timber. This involves cutting trees down to ground level, from where they regrow strong, straight stems. These stems would have been used to make goods, for building, and to make the charcoal needed for working iron. Coppicing tends to extend the life of the trees, and makes an incredibly biodiverse woodland.

CARDONESS CASTLE

Cardoness is an excellent example of a Scottish tower house castle. It was built in the late 15th century by the McCullochs as a family home. It was designed to impress and is similar in style to Threave Castle, built 100 years earlier. It has a two-storey prison cell and a fine dining room, topped with a bed chamber that once filled an entire floor.

It was also designed to protect, which is a good thing when your family is as colourful as the McCullochs, known for their lawlessness. They feuded with their neighbours, the Gordons, and were understandably upset that the Gordons bought the tower house when they were forced to sell. Perhaps not so understandably, Godfrey McCulloch then felt it appropriate to shoot and kill John Gordon. At this point, the McCullochs found they were not above the law; Godfrey was executed for his crimes.

At one time, there would have been a perimeter wall and other buildings where the owners conducted their business, but these have now largely disappeared. The castle is not linked to Cally Castle on the far side of the river, which was built later by another family.

WALK DETAILS

START/FINISH
Gatehouse of Fleet High Street car park, DG7 2HS

DISTANCE
10.5km (6½ miles)

PARKING
At start

PUBLIC TRANSPORT
Bus from Stranraer or Dumfries to Mill on the Fleet

REFRESHMENTS
Pubs and cafés in Gatehouse of Fleet

TOILETS
At start

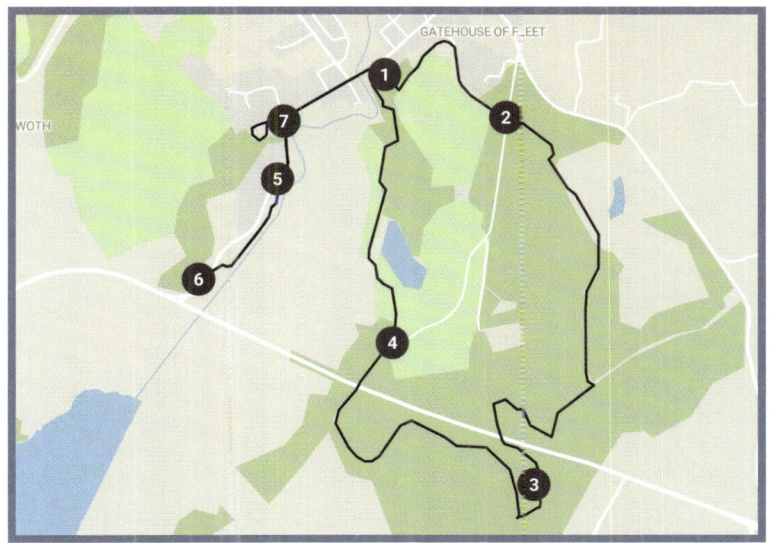

THE WALK

A gentle walk through deciduous woodlands, including a view of Cardoness Castle across the valley. The second leg follows the river to the castle and a viewpoint. Due to a lack of landmarks in the woods, we recommend downloading the GPX file for this walk in case you stray from the route.

LEFT Cardoness Castle (credit: Heartland Arts/Shutterstock).

BELOW Cardoness Castle from a distance.

1 From the car park, take the path straight into the woods between stone gateposts and two boulders. Once you reach the playing field, turn left past the pavilion and continue to skirt the field to a wide gate. Continue ahead on the track on the far side. Turn right behind the bowling clubhouse, then continue ahead around a pair of gates along a stone track. After some time, this leads to a tarmac lane.

2 Cross and continue ahead. After about 30m (33yds), turn left and

then immediately right onto a woodland path that initially runs parallel to the track. At a junction of paths, continue ahead over a small ravine. At the T-junction a few metres further along, turn right and cross a bridge to a stone track. Turn left onto the track. At the junction ahead, continue straight over on another stone track as it skirts the edge of the wood and then bends back into it.

After about a kilometre (⅔ mile), the track reaches a T-junction. Turn right. After some time, the track ends at a path about 30m (33yds) from a fence along the road cutting. Turn right onto a woodland path uphill. The next junction of paths is a crossroads.

Turn left downhill. You will shortly arrive at another T-junction of paths. Turn left. This path winds its way along to a stream then a subway under the A-road and into the woods on the other side. The path bends to the right, away from the road, then follow it to the right to the temple.

The temple was built as a folly in the gardens of Cally House.

3 Continue along the footpath on the far side of the temple. After a short distance, turn right at the crossroads onto a stone path, over a small ravine and to a track.

Turn right and follow this track until you reach a tarmac lane. Turn right, back under the A-road and to the Cally Palace Hotel.

4 Take the path to the left just before the hotel's portico, towards the lake.

Rutherford's Monument is visible on the skyline to your left.
 Back in the trees, when you reach the fourth tee, look to your left to see the remains of Cally Castle. In the distance, there's a fantastic view of Cardoness Castle, too.

At the end of this tee, the path kinks left and then right, over a track and along the side of another fairway before heading back into the woods. When it leaves the woods again, turn right over a stone bridge. After another few metres, turn left at the

crossroads of paths. At the next junction, fork left then left again to the banks of the river. Follow this path over a small wooden bridge to the car park, which marks the end of this section of the walk.

The second loop takes you along the river to the castle. Turn left and cross the Fleet river. Continue along the road past the houses. Pass the left-hand bend, then look for the next tarmac drive on the right.

5 Take the path to the left signposted Cardoness Castle. On reaching the road, cross and ascend the steps to the castle.

6 Return along the same riverside path. At the road, turn right and follow it until you reach the right-hand bend.

7 Take a short detour here to the top of Venniehill by turning left up the grassy path and following the path in a circle around the top. Return to the road by the same route, and retrace your steps along the road back to the start.

ABOVE The Temple.
BELOW Gatehouse of Fleet.

8 CARISBROOKE CASTLE

Carisbrooke Castle is in the middle of the Isle of Wight – a strategically important position for defending both the island and mainland Britain. The Normans built a castle here on an old Saxon enclosure. Over the centuries, it has acted as a fortification, royal palace and prison.

Shortly after the castle's construction in the late 11th century, the Isle of Wight became a stronghold of Empress Matilda, who claimed that she was the rightful heir to the throne of England. King Stephen arrived at the castle with his army to assert his position as king – and found the gates wide open. At that time, the only water in the castle was from a well in the keep. This was purely filled by rainwater and had run dry. The castle's defenders knew

BELOW **Carisbrooke Castle gatehouse.**

WALK DETAILS

START/FINISH
Carisbrooke Castle car park, PO30 1XY

DISTANCE
9.5km (6 miles)

PARKING
At start and Carisbrooke Priory car park PO30 1YS (join at Point 2)

PUBLIC TRANSPORT
Bus from Newport to Carisbrooke High Street or The Waverley

REFRESHMENTS
Pubs and cafés in Carisbrooke, café in castle

TOILETS
In castle

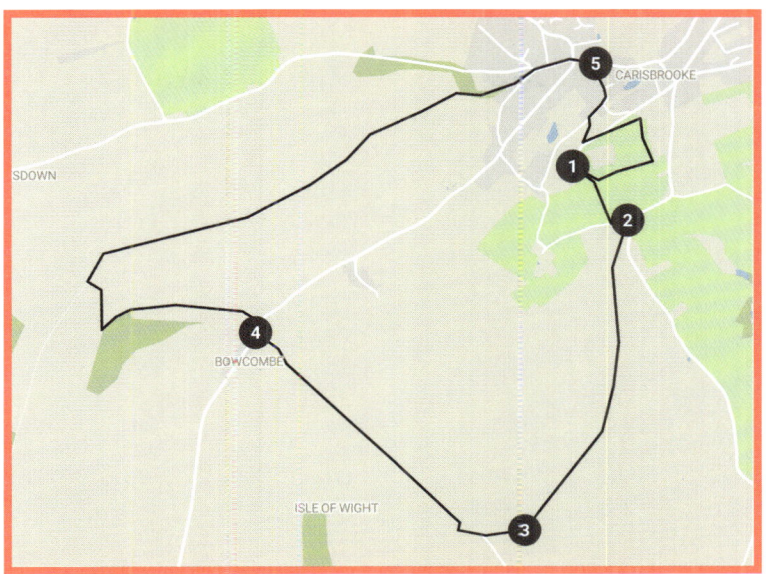

they would quickly succumb to dehydration, so they surrendered.

In response, King Stephen ordered that a new well be dug. This one would be deep enough to reach the aquifer below. Enormous buckets of water were raised, first by prisoners walking on a tread wheel, then donkeys. Donkeys still reside in the castle and demonstrate the operation of the well.

For fine views, visitors can walk around the top of the keep and castle walls.

THE WALK

A moderately difficult walk with several steep ascents, along paths that are well waymarked and maintained. Walk along shady sunken lanes, traverse wide open arable fields and follow the ridge of Bowcombe Down. Great views of the castle within its landscape. Many of the paths are shared with cyclists. Two stiles.

BELOW A section of the route.

1 From the car park, walk towards the castle, then turn right along the wide grass band, heading downhill. The castle walls are on your left. At the bottom of the slope, turn right steeply downhill, following a public footpath sign. At the junction of paths, head straight downhill between hedges. At the end of the hedges, continue straight ahead steeply uphill to a tarmac lane. Turn left onto the lane and look left for a view of the castle. Continue to a T-junction.

2 At the T-junction, turn right along a public bridleway signposted Shepherds Trail. After around 1km (2/3 mile), the path opens out along the edge of a field. At a clear junction of paths a little way ahead, turn right. You are now leaving the Shepherds Trail. Continue to a track.

3 On reaching the track, turn right. At the next junction, turn right onto a tarmac lane, which ends after about 100m (330ft). Bear right around the end of the buildings and stay on the track as it bends left between arable fields.

As you head down towards the hamlet, look right for a good view of the castle.

Eventually, the track passes through a farm, becomes a tarmac drive and reaches a road.

4 Dogleg right and then left to take a footpath, signposted Cow Lane. This is a lovely sunken path between hedges. When the path reaches a gate into a field, pass through the gate and turn sharp right to follow the track uphill. At the top of the hill, turn right onto the farm track, following signs for the Tennyson Trail. At the next junction of paths, continue straight ahead, again on the Tennyson Trail. Although fairly narrow, this is also the Chalk Ridge Extreme cycle path – be aware of fast-moving cyclists. Eventually, the path opens up with views over the valley on the right, including the castle. Shortly after this, the path again has a hedgerow on each side and gently drops into the town. When you reach a tarmac lane, continue heading downhill. At the road, cross to continue downhill on the pavement until you reach St Mary's Church.

5 Opposite the church, turn right along Castle Street. Look up for a view of the castle keep ahead. At the end of Castle Street, cross a small bridge and walk along the stream, then follow the tarmac road ahead. After 140m (150yds), opposite house number 18, take a public footpath left, signposted Carisbrooke Castle. Cross the stile. And then head diagonally right, uphill, to another stile in the corner of the field. Take the steps up to the road near the entrance to the castle. The route turns left here to circumnavigate the castle, giving a good view of the defences. Alternatively, turn right to head straight back to the car park.

The walls nearest to you as you circumnavigate the castle were built around the turn of the 17th century, during the reign of Elizabeth I. They brought the castle's defences right up to date, in order to defend against an anticipated Spanish invasion. The walls have thick banks behind them, so that they would withstand attack by cannon ball, and the shape is designed to fire at an invading army from many different angles. The circular holes were added later as a decorative feature.

Some of these walls are quite some distance from the bailey walls. Originally, this area contained defensive earthworks. Later, during the imprisonment here of Charles I before his execution, it was made into a bowling green for his entertainment.

LEFT The Elizabethan defences.

BELOW Carisbrooke Castle in the landscape.

9 CARLISLE CASTLE

Carlisle has been a military stronghold for nearly 2,000 years. The Romans built a fort on the site of the present castle as early as the 1st century AD, and the town Luguvalium continued to grow until they left 300 years later. The site remained the centre of a Northumbrian royal estate, with the Roman walls still standing. The Vikings arrived 500 years after the Romans left, and the town changed hands several times between the Norse, the Scots and the Britons.

After that, it was time for the Normans to arrive following their conquest of England in 1066. Initially, they built a wooden palisade above the River Eden, followed by a stone castle in the early 12th century. Parts of the Roman fort were reused for the new castle, resulting in some unusual features for a Catholic building, such as a dedication to the gods Jupiter, Juno, Minerva, Mars and Victory on one of the doorway lintels. As it is in such a strategic location, Carlisle remained a disputed territory, and the castle again changed hands several times between Scottish and Anglo-Norman owners.

The castle continued to be used for military purposes on and off until the middle of the 20th century, and the British military retains a presence here even now.

WALK DETAILS

START/FINISH
Carlisle railway station, CA1 1QZ

DISTANCE
9.5km (6 miles)

PARKING
Sheepmount car park at castle, car parks in Carlisle

PUBLIC TRANSPORT
Train to Carlisle

REFRESHMENTS
Pubs and cafés in Carlisle, café in castle

TOILETS
In castle and Carlisle library

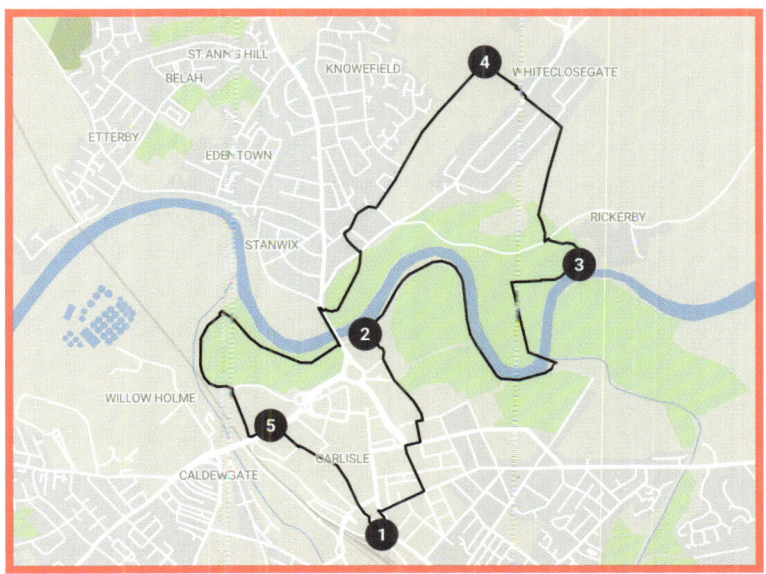

THE WALK

An easy walk with many fascinating features. Learn about the huge losses of WWI at the war memorial, and about the local geology at the stone circle. Walk in the footsteps of Roman soldiers along the route of Hadrian's Wall (dismantled) and through a river meadow right into the city.

LEFT Carlisle Castle gatehouse.

BELOW The river meadow.

1 From the main station entrance, walk straight ahead past the citadel towers. At the traffic lights, turn right onto Warwick Road. When you reach the crossroads at Spencer Street, turn left. At the next large junction, turn right onto Victoria Place, then take the first left onto Compton Street. At the end, turn right, and then almost immediately left down a cycle path to the right of the leisure centre. Continue in the same direction until you reach the river.

CARLISLE CASTLE

The large wooden post marks a sculpture representing all the forts along the length of Hadrian's Wall.

2 Turn right along the river. Cross at the steel footbridge. From the bridge, look left for a view of the castle keep. Continue ahead to the cenotaph. Turn right onto the grassy path, then when you reach the river, turn left to the stone circle that depicts the geological history of the Eden Valley.

3 Turn away from the river and proceed to a car park. Cross the road and take the footpath signposted Longlands Road. Pass through two gates and follow the path diagonally right across a meadow. Pass through the gate on the far side, and walk straight ahead through the housing estate. At the end of the road, dogleg right then left onto the footpath along the edge of a field.

After about 20m (65ft), you will cross the line of Vallum, a ditch that ran close to Hadrian's Wall, although it is not visible today.

At the end of the field, pass through a kissing gate, cross a small ditch and turn left.

4 You are now walking along the line of Hadrian's Wall.

This is the position of Milecastle 65. There is nothing left to see, because the stone was used to build Carlisle castle – look out for the stones with crosshatching in the castle walls.

Continue straight. Eventually, the path bends slightly to the left. When you

BELOW Carlisle Castle keep.

reach a road, continue ahead with the University of Cumbria on your left. At the end of the road, turn right and follow this road around to the left. Pass the Crown and Mitre pub, then turn left around the far end of the church and down to the B-road.

> *This is the site of Petriana, a Roman fort that was home to a regiment of 1,000 soldiers.*

Cross into Rickerby Park. Follow the path gently downhill, then turn right through Eden Bridge Garden onto the bridge.

Cross the river. On the far side, turn sharp left and then left again underneath the bridge so the river is on your right. Take the raised footpath straight ahead. At the junction, fork right. The castle is now visible to your left beyond the tennis courts.

As you reach the car park at the end of the raised avenue, detour right towards the river then left at the parallel bars to see stones from the base of the Roman bridge that were recovered from the river.

Turn left at the car park. The castle tower is now visible on your left. Once you reach the next car park, walk to the right around the castle walls to the entrance.

5 On leaving the castle, continue straight ahead along Castle Street. Pass the Tullie Museum and then the cathedral At the market square, bear right and continue ahead at the end of the pedestrian precinct.

> *The stone arches and the two round towers are replicas of the old citadel walls built in the 19th century.*

The station is a short distance further on the right.

BELOW The stone circle that depicts the geological history of the Eden Valley.

10 CASTELL BIWMARES
BEAUMARIS CASTLE

Castell Biwmares was to be the jewel in the crown of Edward I's fortifications to control the Welsh. Because it was built on flat land, it was possible to make it completely symmetrical, with three lines of defence – a moat, a wall and the castle itself. In case of siege by land, a short canal was dug from the Menai Strait to a defended dock to allow the resupply of essential goods.

By the time Castell Biwmares was under construction, Edward's attention was being drawn to Scotland, and he started to run out of money for his ambitious projects. Over 3,000 men were employed to build the castle. By February 1296, the king was behind with payments to both men and suppliers. Building work slowed that year after the invasion of Scotland, and some of the buildings planned for within the castle were never completed. The towers did not achieve their full planned height. This is part of the castle's charm. As it was never finished, it was also never modernised, and what we see now is almost exactly how it was when it was built.

The chapel has beautiful stained-glass windows and incredible acoustics. Why not try singing here and see whether you agree?

WALK DETAILS

START/FINISH
Beaumaris Castle, LL58 8AP

DISTANCE
9.5km (6 miles)

PARKING
Car park at start

PUBLIC TRANSPORT
Train to Bangor, then bus to Castle Street, Beaumaris

REFRESHMENTS
Pubs and cafés in Beaumaris

TOILETS
In Beaumaris

BELOW The moat, curtain wall and towers (credit: Crown copyright (2023) Cymru Wales).

THE WALK

A varied walk along a boulder-strewn beach, past other-worldly rock formations, through woodland to another castle and back across fields, a golf course and a quiet lane with tremendous views of the castle. Easy walking, but slow along the beach, with some uphill sections. It has one dog-proof stile.

BELOW The beach between Points 2 and 3.

CASTELL BIWMARES ■ BEAUMARIS CASTLE

1 **With your back to the castle, turn left to join the coast path,** keeping the Menai Strait to your right.

When the path joins the road, continue for some time until the road bends away from the water to the left.

2 **Turn right onto the beach, then left along the shore.**
NOTE: This part of the route is not safe to walk within one hour each side of high tide. If necessary, follow the alternative route on the sign and rejoin the walk at Point 3.

The beach is rocky and slow-going, but enjoyable nonetheless. After some time, you will pass some dramatic sandstone cliff formations containing sand martin nests.

Shortly after these and before a stream, turn left to cross the stream and reach the road. Turn left onto the road, cross the stream again, then turn right onto the footpath. Follow to a track.

3 **Turn right then right again signposted to the castle, over a long wooden bridge.** Where the path forks, turn right up a wooden boardwalk. At the end of the boardwalk, continue straight ahead. At the next junction, continue straight ahead, signposted entrance. A few metres further, turn left over a wooden bridge and up a flight of steps to Castell Aberlleiniog.

The original castle here predates Castell Biwmares by about 200 years.

Retrace your steps down to the path, turn right at the bottom, over the bridge, left at the fork then back down the boardwalk.

At the bottom of the boardwalk, turn right and follow the stony path through the woodland until you reach a few stone steps down to a concrete lane. Turn left and follow the lane to a house on the right. Turn right immediately after the house, then continue straight ahead onto a woodland path.

At a kissing gate, turn left downhill onto a narrow path between gardens. At another kissing gate, continue back into woods with a stream on your left. Eventually, you will reach a short flight of stone steps to a road.

4 **Turn left along the road, cross the stream and after a few more metres, take a footpath on the right.** Cross the stile into a caravan park. Turn left towards the caravans and then along the tarmac drive between them. At a fork in the drive with clear footpath signs, bear right and right again to the kissing gate and into a field.

Bear diagonally left to a gap in the hedge on the far side, heading towards the obelisk visible on the

horizon. Head straight across the next field, still towards the obelisk, to a lane opposite the entrance to Plas Cichle. Turn left onto the lane into Llanfaes, a hamlet with a church.

5 Follow the lane to the right, then almost immediately turn left. Pass Llanfaes Lodge on your right, then take the footpath diagonally right through stone gateposts onto the golf course. Cross the first fairway then follow the yellow-topped posts in a more or less straight line across the golf course to a lane. When passing ponds on the right, the next post may not be visible – continue in the same direction uphill with the fairway on your right.

At the lane on the far side of the golf course, turn right then follow the road to the left down the slope back into Beaumaris. There are excellent views of the castle from this road.

6 When you reach the town, turn left, then left twice more to reach the castle and the end of the walk.

ABOVE The gatehouse (credit: Crown copyright (2023) Cymru Wales).

BELOW The castle as seen between Points 5 and 6.

CASTELL CAERDYDD
CARDIFF CASTLE

The glory of Castell Caerdydd is threefold.

First, it is the only Roman fort in Britain that has been rebuilt. Once the old Roman walls were discovered, the 3rd Marquess of Bute excavated the Norman earth banks that had hidden them. He then reconstructed the walls as accurately as he knew, with one modification – the addition of a gallery so that he could exercise inside in bad weather.

Second, the Norman keep, raised on its motte and surrounded by a moat, is considered the finest in Wales. The rest of the Norman castle was removed when the grounds were remodelled by 'Capability' Brown in the 1770s.

Finally, the renovations by the 3rd Marquess of Bute in the late 19th century have resulted in a magnificent stately home within the castle's walls. Every image and carving seems to have meaning, including a monkey carved into a door arch in the library with the face of Darwin, as a protest against the theory of evolution. There is also a sense of joy and levity, including scenes from children's stories depicted in a frieze in the nursery and the life cycle of the clothes moth carved into his wardrobe.

RIGHT The Norman keep.

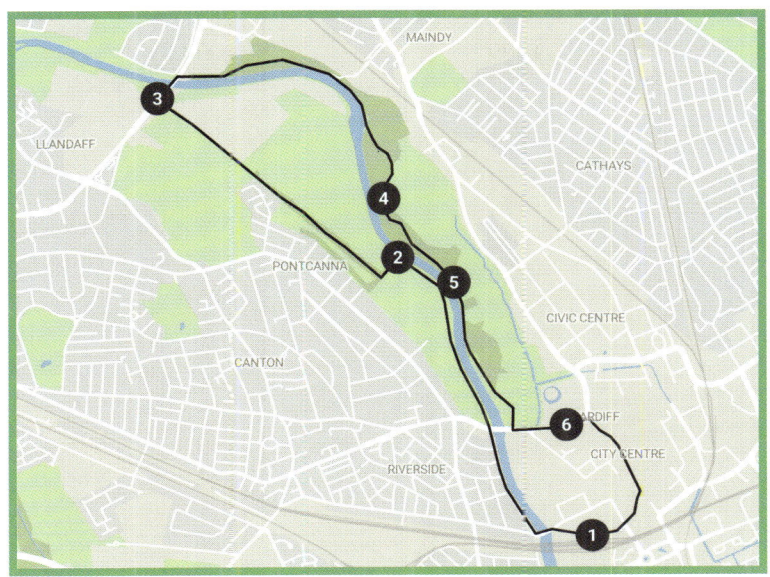

THE WALK

Discover the lively waters of the River Taff, as well as the arboretum and woodland walk in Bute Park. This is an easy walk that mainly follows tarmac paths, with options to shorten if desired. Walking boots are not required. The city centre will be busy on match days at the Principality Stadium.

1 **From the station's front concourse, turn left as you exit,** taking note of the modern mosaics built into the station wall. Turn left again onto the road at the end of One Central Square, to cross the River Taff. On the far side of the bridge, turn right to follow the river upstream.

Continue on this path for around 1.5km (1 mile). You will pass the Principality Stadium, home of Welsh rugby, on the far side of the river. You can choose to pass under or over the road at Cardiff Bridge, staying on the same side of the river. (At the footbridge, you can cross to return to the route between Points 5 and 6. There is also a café on the far side.) The full route continues

WALK DETAILS

START/FINISH
Cardiff Central railway station, CF10 1EP

DISTANCE
8km (5 miles)

PARKING
City centre, or Sophia Gardens CF11 9SZ to join at the footbridge between Points 1 & 2

PUBLIC TRANSPORT
Train to Cardiff Central or coach to Sophia Gardens

REFRESHMENTS
Café on east side of the first footbridge, at Point 5 and on leaving Bute Park

TOILETS
On the west side of the first footbridge

CASTELL CAERDYDD ■ *CARDIFF CASTLE*

upstream and runs between the river and the Sophia Gardens stadium, home of Glamorgan Cricket.

2 At the end of the stadium, turn left down the far side of a stone wall, along a row of evergreen holm oaks.

(To shorten the walk by just over 1km (⅔ mile), continue along the riverside path and cross the river at Blackweir footbridge.)

At the road, turn right down a long avenue of lime trees. Continue around 1.5km (1 mile) to the end of the avenue.

3 Pass through the gates, then head right along the road to cross the river again. Once on the other side, drop down to the right to join the tarmac path, this time heading downstream. Follow the path past the footbridge at Blackweir and through a wood, with an arboretum on the left, to a playing field.

Although the trees here are young (mainly planted in 1947), many are rare, making this arboretum significant in the UK. Not all the trees are big like the ones alongside the path – the arboretum also contains collections of crab apple, rowan, alder and hawthorn.

4 With the playing field on your left, take one of the narrow paths on the right, then turn left onto the woodland trail, marked with posts. (If you would prefer to stay on tarmac, continue on the path, keeping right at each junction.)

The river is now on your right, on the other side of a low bank. Do not be tempted to cross the bank to walk by the water, as the trees next to the river are being left to decline naturally, which means there's a risk of falling branches.

CASTELL CAERDYDD ■ *CARDIFF CASTLE*

The woodland path meets the tarmac path again by an old walled garden that now houses a visitor centre.

5 Continue in the same direction, past the footbridge and through a more formal part of the park to the road. Turn left onto the road.

You will pass the Animal Wall, which was designed to show people what these exotic animals are like. In the late 1800s, when the wall was built, most would have been unfamiliar with creatures such as lions, baboons and anteaters. Originally, the animals were painted in naturalistic colours, although over time the paint has faded and not been replaced.

ABOVE The remains of the Roman walls, visible below the rebuilt wall.

LEFT Bute Park

The castle entrance is a little further along on the left.

6 As you leave the castle from the same entrance, turn left to the end of the fortification. Cross the road to turn right down St John Street, past the church of St John the Baptist. Continue through the city centre until you reach the modern library building. Turn right in front of the building and continue ahead, crossing St Mary's Street, until you return to the station concourse.

CASTELL CAERDYDD ■ *CARDIFF CASTLE*

CASTELL CAERFFILI
CAERPHILLY CASTLE

Castell Caerffili is a Norman fortress surrounded by moats, built to protect against the growing influence of the newly crowned Prince of Wales, Llywelyn ap Gruffudd. Construction started in 1268, and in a few years, it was complete. Once Edward I defeated Llywelyn a few years later, the castle was turned into a residence designed to flaunt the power of its new owner, Gilbert de Clare. Painted white, it would have been mightily conspicuous and visible from afar.

Despite its opulence, the castle fell out of favour with its owners after less than a century of use and fell into disrepair. Its decay was accelerated during the British Civil Wars in the 1640s and by the sale of some of its stone to build a local mansion.

By the early 20th century, it was a ruin. The 3rd Marquess of Bute reroofed the great hall, and then his son, the 4th marquess, spent a fortune on rebuilding work. He seems to have been driven by social conscience, employing 15 masons for 12 years, just as the work was needed, after the general strike of 1926 and

WALK DETAILS

START/FINISH
Caerphilly railway station, CF83 1JR

DISTANCE
9.25km (5¾ miles)

PARKING
At start

PUBLIC TRANSPORT
Train or bus to Caerphilly

REFRESHMENTS
Pubs and cafés in Caerphilly

TOILETS
In Café Tyfu near the station, castle, library, visitor centre

during the Great Depression. The work cost over £100,000, which equates to more than £6.5 million today.

THE WALK
Much of this walk is through delightful broadleaf wood and that is carpeted with wildflowers in spring. The final leg climbs to the top of Caerphilly Common. From here, there are excellent views of the castle and, more distantly, Cardiff Bay. The path is often muddy and is uneven in places.

1 From the station, head towards the road bridge then turn right onto Cardiff Road downhill through the town.

2 If you are visiting the castle, turn left into Dafydd Williams Park when the castle comes into view and turn right around the moat to the entrance. If not, continue to the Tommy Cooper statue, then follow the road between the community centre and library. Cross the road ahead onto Van Road. Continue to the roundabout. Head straight over.

LEFT The castle and its moat.

ABOVE A view from Caerphilly Common.
LEFT The statue of Tommy Cooper.

After 150m (165yds), turn left into a residential cul-de-sac. At the end of the houses, continue straight ahead. Turn left at the road and stay on this pavement until it reaches Caerphilly Woods car park.

3 **Take the track from the car park that runs uphill, and after 125m (137yds),** turn right through a series of BMX cycle tracks. At the end, head through the gap in the fence onto a smaller path, and turn right at the junction. This path shortly reaches a road. Follow the road to the left for less than 100m (110yds) before turning right at the lime kilns. Here, take the left fork along a forestry track, until you reach a small pond. Continue with the pond on your left, where the path rises, through coppiced broadleaf woodland, to a T-junction of paths.

4 **Turn right.** After some time, the path bends to the left and through a horse gate just before it meets a track. Turn right here, and after about 20m (65ft), take the left fork that gently rises. As the path meets another from the left, it joins the Cambrian Way and Rhymney Valley Ridgeway Walk. At the next junction, turn right. This path runs along the edge of lovely woodland for some distance before reaching a road.

5 **Turn left along the verge, then cross the road to take the path at the end of the buildings.** This is still signposted the Cambrian Way and has a small stream on the left. At a long cottage, walk to the left of the building, then to the left of the agricultural shed to a golf course. About 30m (100ft) ahead, turn right at the waymarker, then follow more waymarkers onto a narrow path through a wood, across a stream and then across a fairway.

At the kissing gate, head directly

62 CASTELL CAERFFILI ■ *CAERPHILLY CASTLE*

ABOVE Lime kilns.

uphill. Near the top of the rise, turn left at the waymarker, following the line of the pylons through young woodland. At the next junction, turn right at the waymarker to continue to follow the pylons. Stay on this path until you reach a road.

6 Turn right onto the minor road, then cross the A-road and take the path directly ahead onto Caerphilly Common. After about 25m (80ft), fork left and follow this narrow path to the top of the Caerphilly Mountain and trig point.

> From here, there's a fantastic view of the castle ahead and to the left. Behind and to the right, the view extends across Cardiff Bay.

7 From the trig point, head down towards the castle and follow the broad path to the right around the hill. On the far side of the hill, at the first significant junction, turn left. In a dip between hills, take a footpath on the left that heads gently downhill towards a wooded valley.

Fork right just before the trees. At the golf course, turn right across the grass, then right again down a track that becomes a path skirting the edge of the course. When this path reaches the road, turn left back into the centre of Caerphilly and the station.

CASTELL CAERNARFON

Castell Caernarfon was built to impress. After defeating the Welsh princes in 1282, King Edward I decided to construct a new fortress-palace on the site of the old Norman timber motte and bailey castle. His palace was built with multangular towers and walls with coloured bands in the style of the Roman walls of Constantinople. This was to become the administrative centre of North Wales, so the town walls were built contemporaneously to protect the English administrators, builders, mariners and merchants. They were breached by the Welsh in 1294 and had to be rebuilt in places, but they remain intact today, and it is possible to walk around them at ground level.

A ring of castles, including Castell Caernarfon, was constructed around the Welsh stronghold of Snowdonia to quell any rebellion. As such, it was well defended. It featured unique multiple arrow-loops, allowing three archers to fire a deluge of arrows

WALK DETAILS

START/FINISH
Aber Foreshore Road, Caernarfon LL54 5RR

DISTANCE
8.75km (5½ miles)

PARKING
On road at start. If the swing bridge opposite the castle is open, you can start in the castle car park, walk to the far end of the quay and follow the path alongside the steam railway to join the main route at Point 2

PUBLIC TRANSPORT
Train to Bangor, bus to bus station

REFRESHMENTS
Pubs and cafés in Caernarfon. Café at Fron Goch Garden Centre between Points 2 & 3

TOILETS
In castle, next to castle car park

through just one arrow-loop on the outside of the wall.

The first English Prince of Wales, ruler of all the Crown's Welsh lands, was born in Castell Caernarfon in 1284. In 1911, and then again in 1969, the Prince of Wales was invested in the castle, continuing the royal connection.

THE WALK

An easy walk largely along quiet country lanes and the side of a steam railway. Excellent views of the

LEFT The coloured bands and multangular towers of the castle as seen from between Points 1 and 2.

BELOW The slate quay.

CASTELL CAERNARFON ■ *CAERNARFON CASTLE*

ABOVE A steam train on the Welsh Highland Railway.

mountains of Snowdonia, across the Menai Strait to Anglesey, and of the castle from the east (seaward side) and south. If you time it right, you might also see a steam train passing.

1 Walk towards the castle, with the sea on your left. From here, you have a splendid view of the Eagle Tower and the town walls.

The Eagle Tower is the grandest of the castle's towers. It has ten sides and its proportions and three turrets make it stand apart from the others. The battlements and turrets are adorned with stone figures. Most are helmeted heads, and at least one is of the tower's namesake – an eagle. The tower is no longer on the seafront, but visitors were once able to enter its basement by boat.

Follow the road past the footbridge and gently uphill.

From here, you can see the different-coloured bands of stone, one of the design features replicated from the Roman walls of Constantinople. As the road bends to the right and uphill, you start to see vaccary walls made from vertical pieces of slate, partially buried in the ground.

Just before the next right-hand bend in the road, look to your left for a magnificent view of the castle. From here, you can see just how large and impressive it is. There is no indication that Edward I ran out of money, so couldn't finish building it.

Cross the railway. At the end of the road, turn right up another road heading uphill and follow this to the railway crossing.

2 Cross the tracks and continue walking in the same direction, with the tracks on your left.

In the 19th century, the construction of the railway into Caernarfon brought prosperity to the town. The station was sited next to the slate quay, which enabled the slate export trade to flourish. The Welsh Highland Railway that now runs along the tracks is the longest heritage railway in the UK, running for 40km (25 miles) from Caernarfon to Porthmadog.

If you fancy a break, turn right after about 400m (¼ mile), then left to the Fron Goch Garden Centre and its café. Continue along the railway until you reach Bontnewydd.

3 Cross the tracks and head downhill, then right under the railway bridge on a quiet lane. Head straight over the crossroads and continue along the lane for another 1.5km (1 mile) or so. Eventually, the tarmac lane becomes a stone drive. Continue to Plas Farm.

4 Immediately after the farmhouse, turn right past the barns and onto a grassy track between hedges. At the end of this track, take a look around at the mountain views, then turn left through a small garden gate and follow the path past two houses down to the sea.

5 Turn right along the coast road back to the starting point.

This is one of the widest points of the Menai Strait that runs between mainland Wales and the island of Anglesey. Because the Menai Strait is long, narrow and tidal, strong currents surge and swirl through the gap, creating dangerous conditions for boats. In this area, the issue is compounded by sandbanks that shift around, making the position of the channel unpredictable.

In this part of Wales, you might hear people chatting in Welsh as they go about their daily business. According to the 2021 census, over 60 per cent of people here can speak Welsh, and for many it remains the language of choice.

ABOVE The Eagle Tower.

CASTELL CAERNARFON ■ CAERNARFON CASTLE

14 CASTELL CARREG CENNEN

Castell Carreg Cennen perches on a limestone crag high above the Cennen valley. Views extend east across the near reaches of the Brecon Beacons. Below, the valley's fertile land gives some clue about why the castle might have been built here.

A castle was first built on this site by a Welsh prince, taken by the English and then recovered in 1248. Less than 30 years later, it was back in English control. Architectural details indicate that the castle we see today was built contemporaneously with the Ring of Iron in North Wales after the defeat of the Welsh princes by Edward I in 1282–3.

Although the vertical rock face and entrance guarded by multiple drawbridges and two portcullises make the castle appear unassailable, it did fall again during Owain Glyndŵr's revolt in the early 1400s.

Its last hurrah was during the Wars of the Roses when it was taken for the final time in 1462 and demolished, leaving what we see today.

The cave under the outer ward remains a curiosity. Whatever the reason for its existence, it's a great place to explore – as long as you are sure-footed and not afraid of the dark.

THE WALK
This walk leads to stunning views of the castle from across the valley, showing its prominence in the landscape. The route crosses and follows several lively streams. It is well waymarked, although moderately challenging, with multiple stiles and a couple of steep ascents. Muddy in places. Sometimes uneven underfoot.

WALK DETAILS

START/FINISH
Carreg Cennen Castle car park, Trapp SA19 6UA

DISTANCE
5.75km (3½ miles)

PARKING
At start

PUBLIC TRANSPORT
None

REFRESHMENTS
Café at start

TOILETS
In café

BELOW Carreg Cennen occupies a fine defensive position.

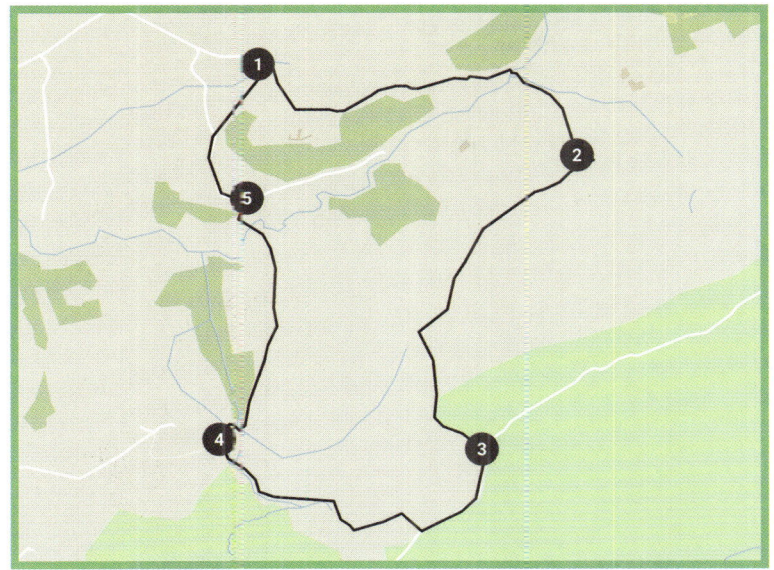

1 Walk through the farm. Pick up your ticket here, if you are planning to visit the castle. By the shed at the entrance to the castle grounds where the path leads up to the castle, turn left downhill into Carreg Cennen Woods.

> These woods are unusual because a geological fault runs through them, leaving two different bedrocks: limestone and sandstone. Each supports different species – limestone favours ash trees and sandstone favours oaks. The woods are an SSSI and a Local Nature Reserve because this is such an important habitat.

Follow the path down into the valley, across two streams and up the other side to where the path ends at a junction of tracks.

2 Cross the stile and head uphill, diagonally left. Follow this track around to the right along the slope, with the valley below to your right. Where the track turns back on itself

ABOVE The castle and one of the stiles between Points 4 and 5.

to the left, continue straight ahead with the valley still to your right.

> There are fabulous views of the castle from this stretch of the route.

CASTELL CARREG CENNEN ■ CARREG CENNEN CASTLE

Where the path ends at two farm gates, cross the stile and follow the waymarkers across the corner of a field then along the hedge on your right. At the end of the hedge, head to the left of a stand of trees, to another stile.

Cross this stile and follow the fenced path past an agricultural shed. When it reaches the farm drive, continue away from the farm until you reach a tarmac lane.

3 **Turn right onto the lane for about 400m (440yds).** At the end of a drystone wall on the right, cross the stile and head to the left of the shake hole ahead. At the next stile, turn left between another two shake holes, following the waymarkers.

ABOVE The River Loughor between Points 3 and 4.

Shake holes are formed where the layer of boulder clay above limestone is washed down into the rock, leaving a depression on the surface. As you can see, these can be quite deep and steep-sided.

There is a clear path across the field, which then becomes a track and meanders down to the right. You will hear a stream down to your left. Cross another stile and follow the line of the stream, past redundant watercress beds.

This is the River Loughor, which eventually forms a wide estuary on the north side of the Gower Peninsula. If you see watercress growing in a stream, it's a sign of clean water, as the plant does not tolerate pollution well. However, if you pick it wild, it's still a good idea to wash it well before eating.

Stay on the track until you reach a stile.

4 Cross the stile and head downhill on a stony track, over another stream and up the far side. As you walk, the castle will come into view high up ahead. When the path reaches a garden, turn left and cross the field, heading downhill to the left of the castle. The gate you are heading for soon becomes visible. Pass through this gate and continue downhill to the left, to another footbridge. Cross the field ahead and another stile, then climb a long flight of steps. At the top, there's yet another stile to cross before heading

ABOVE An old track along the river between Points 3 and 4.

BELOW The castle as seen from between Points 2 and 3.

diagonally left across the field to a gate that leads to the road.

5 Turn left onto the road for about 300m (330yds). At a gate, turn right and cross to the far left-hand corner of the field to one side of the visitor centre and café. Turn left to return to the car park, or right for well-earned refreshments.

CASTELL CAS-GWENT
CHEPSTOW CASTLE

Castell Cas-Gwent was built by William the Conqueror and his allies early in his reign, at a similar time to the Tower of London. The River Wye formed the border between Wales and England, so the castle's position on the west side of the river – the Welsh side – was probably a strategic move and a strong statement of power.

Whatever the reason for the choice of site, the castle is undoubtedly in a spectacular position, perched along the top of a cliff on the bed on the river. The great tower is the oldest part of the castle. Look out for the saltire-patterned lintel and arch, typical of Norman buildings. The tower was built reusing stone from Caerwent, a ruined Roman village nearby. The most obvious element is the band of orange tiles running across the east wall. Somewhat less obvious is the carving on the south wall that is thought to be of Venus.

Another remarkable feature of the castle is the number of ancient doors that have survived. Some are as much

WALK DETAILS

START/FINISH
Castle Dell car park, NP16 5GA

DISTANCE
8.75km (5½ miles)

PARKING
At start

PUBLIC TRANSPORT
Train or coach to Chepstow

REFRESHMENTS
Pubs and cafés in Chepstow, café in Tutshill

TOILETS
At start

BELOW The castle as seen from the bridge between Points 1 and 2.

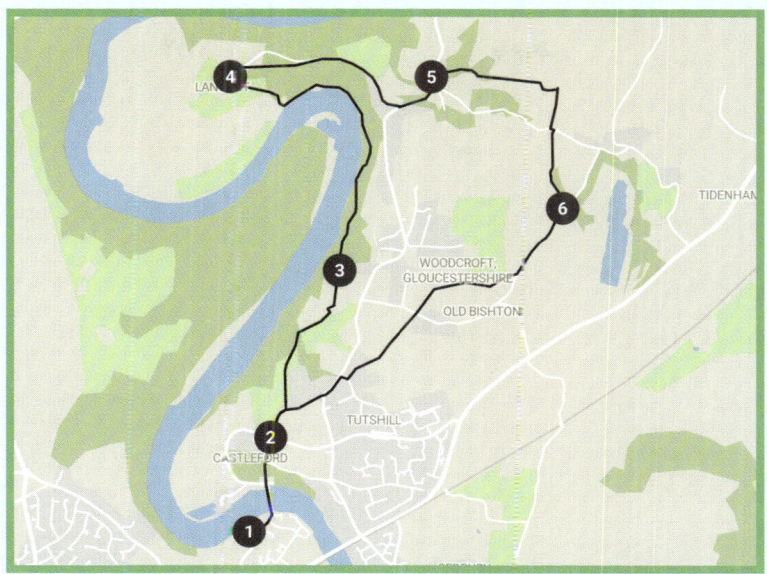

as 500 years old, but these pale into insignificance against the original doors from the main gatehouse, which are over 800 years old.

THE WALK
This is a walk of two halves. The first half is challenging – narrow paths, steep ascents and descents, uneven ground and a boulder field are all encountered while following the line of the tidal river. The second half is far gentler across the hills to the east of Chepstow, but does have some stiles.

1 Head to the road and turn left to cross the bridge over the River Wye. Look out for the view of the castle to the left as you cross. From the far side, take the wide tarmacked footpath straight ahead, uphill, until you reach a road.

LEFT Negotiating the boulder field.

RIGHT The ruins of St James' church.

RIGHT BELOW The castle from the land.

2 Cross the road and continue ahead to join a lane. At a junction of drives, take the path on the left, waymarked Offa's Dyke.

As this path rises, look back over your left shoulder for a view of the castle.

Follow this path to the corner of the field. Walk through two kissing gates, keeping the wall to your left. At the end of this path, turn right along a drive, then left after 35m (38yds). Follow Offa's Dyke straight ahead to another kissing gate.

3 Turn left, duck under a bridge and enter Lancaut Nature Reserve. Follow this narrow path through the woods, waymarked with red arrows. Take your time to cross the boulder field safely.

After the boulder field, the path turns uphill. Where it meets another path, turn left (red arrow). After a bench looking down the river, fork right to avoid a section of path being washed away.

The route eventually leads to the ruins of St James' Church and turns uphill. Near the top of the churchyard wall, fork left to go through a gate and across a field, heading to the right of the farm buildings to a farm gate.

Look behind for a view of the massive limestone cliffs that line the river.

4 Through the gate, turn right onto a lane. About halfway to where the road is fenced, head diagonally right, through a small gate and into woodland. After a few metres, fork left past lime kilns. Continue in approximately the same direction until you rejoin the lane. Turn right along the lane until you reach the B4228. Turn left onto the road and follow it for about 200m (220yds) to a junction.

5 Just beyond the junction, take the footpath on the right immediately past the bus stop and postbox (ignoring the Offa's Dyke sign). Follow this path between drives, along a garden wall and then between fields. Cross the stile and head down the field with the fence line on your left. Cross the remains of a drystone wall and cross the corner of the field, then bear left around the corner and cross another stile. Turn right downhill. When you reach a lane, dogleg left then right before the bridge. Continue with fields on your right until the path bends to the right to another kissing gate.

6 Pass through the gate, then turn right along the lane, between hedges. After 230m, (250yds) at a

double farm gate, turn right through the kissing gate then left along the track.

The Severn Estuary is visible to the left.

At a junction of tracks, head downhill towards the farm buildings, then right up a track before reaching them. At the end of the fence, cross the stile and follow the path diagonally right across two fields to a farm gate and lane. Cross the lane and continue ahead, through a gate in a hedge then over a stone stile. After a short distance, the path squeezes between back gardens. When you reach a road, turn right then left on the pavement along the more major road. Where this road bends left, cross to continue straight ahead along the quieter Mopla Road. Follow this road back to Point 2 and retrace your steps down the hill, over the bridge and back to the car park.

16 CASTELL COCH

Little is known about the history of Castell Coch, except that it was probably Welsh, not Norman, and that it was built by the end of the 13th century.

What you see today is a Victorian rebuilding of the original. Castell Coch was owned by the same man as Cardiff Castle – the 3rd Marquess of Bute. He used the same architect and interior designer – William Burges – and the similarity in style is evident. Although, in some respects, he seems to have tried to recreate the medieval castle as it was, there are also many flights of fancy. One example is the use of conical roofs on the towers, which is rather more European in style than Welsh. Another is the decoration of the drawing room, which has a domed ceiling (despite having a floor above) and contains illustrations of Aesop's Fables and statues of the three Fates from Greek mythology. Within the wall frieze is a monkey with Darwin's face – also seen in Cardiff Castle (see Walk 11) – mocking the theory of evolution.

WALK DETAILS

START/FINISH
Fforest Fawr car park, Caerphilly CF83 1NG

DISTANCE
9.75km (6 miles)

PARKING
At start

PUBLIC TRANSPORT
Bus from Cardiff to Tongwynlais (join walk at castle), train to Taff's Well (join walk at Point 3)

REFRESHMENTS
Café in castle, pub and café in Tongwynlais

TOILETS
In castle

BELOW The castle entrance (credit: Crown copyright (2023) Cymru Wales).

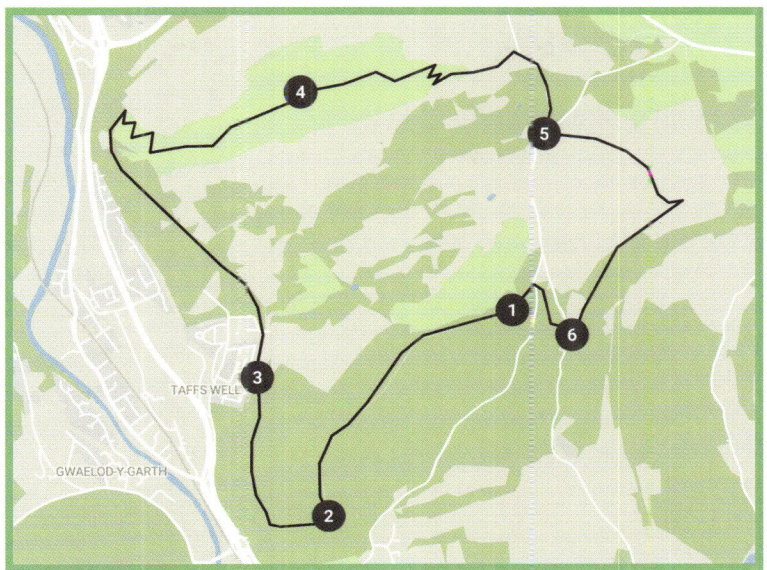

Monkeys also feature in Lady Bute's bedroom above. Most of them are brown, and one is grey. No one knows why, although it is likely to have some meaning that has been lost in time.

THE WALK

This walk is mainly through deciduous woodland. In contrast, the stretch along the ridge of Craig yr Allt has far-reaching views – a reward for the climb up. The final section is muddy – boots are recommended. To avoid the mud, cut along the road from Point 4 to the end. Two stiles.

1 From the top of the car park, pass the barrier to follow the main path with green and brown waymarkers. At a junction of paths, take the left fork.

> When you see a wooden bear on the right, you are at the Three Bears Caves. These are entrances to now disused mines, fenced off for safety.

At a significant crossroads of paths, continue straight ahead, following the red and yellow waymarkers. At this point, the track heads gently uphill and bends to the left. Where the track bears right, continue straight ahead if you wish to visit the castle.

BELOW A wizard in Fforest Fawr.

CASTELL COCH

2 **If you're not visiting the castle, follow the track around to the right, then gently downhill.** Eventually, you will reach some metal barriers with a bridge to your left.

3 **Bear right and then left past the barriers, following the line of the old railway with houses on your left.** Continue on this path for another 1.5km (1 mile) until the path bends right and then left through some more metal barriers. Turn right before the derelict bridge and cross a stile, following the waymarker. After a minute or two, the path bends right and takes wide zigzags up onto the ridge of Craig yr Allt. If you are not sure which is the correct path, don't worry – just head to the top of the hill. As you climb, the views open up to the right over the city of Cardiff and the Bristol Channel. Fork left for one final push to reach the ridge.

4 **Turn right when you get there,** following the ridge line to the high point ahead and onto the eastern end of the hill, where the path drops in another series of wide zigzags. At the tarmac drive, turn left until you reach a minor road. Turn right onto the road for approximately 500m (⅓ mile) to another junction and the Black Cock Inn.

5 **The final section of the walk is likely to be muddy. (To avoid the mud, turn right here and follow the road, keeping right at the junction, to return to the start.)** To continue the route, cross into the car park. Turn left behind the pub to cross a wooden footbridge and a stile. Head diagonally across the field towards a telegraph pole, cross a stile and continue to the far right-hand corner of the next field. Cross the footbridge and a track, then go through another gate. At the barn ahead, turn right over a small bridge and then left towards the gate visible at the end of the field. Through the gate, head for the far right-hand corner of the field. To achieve this, turn right along the fence line and then diagonally left on a fairly clear path. Where this path reaches the fence line, follow it around to the right. This is another muddy section.

CASTELL COCH ■ *COCH CASTLE*

As a minor path merges with this one, keep the fence line on your left until you reach a gate. Through the gate, fork left to and through a kissing gate. The path continues downhill for a short distance, still with a fence line on the left. When it reaches a farm track, turn right onto the track and follow this for about 1km (⅔ mile) to a minor road.

6 Turn right onto the road for about 30m (100ft), then left onto a small footpath that leads straight downhill through beautiful beech woodland. Where it reaches another path, turn right and follow it to another road. You will see the entrance to the car park directly ahead.

ABOVE Part of the route between Points 5 and 6.

BELOW Craig yr Allt ridge.

17 CASTELL CONWY

Edward I moved fast after capturing Aberconwy early in 1283. He arrived in the town on 13 March, and within three or four days, work started on building the castle. The defence of the town, which was planned as an administrative centre for the region, started two months later. It only took four years to complete the construction of the castle and the town walls. Despite this haste, they remain some of Britain's most impressive medieval buildings.

The town walls survive largely intact, with a walkway around the top. The walls have three gates with twin towers and 21 other towers. Towers helped to defend the weaker curtain walls and were used to good effect here in Conwy, in both the town wall and castle. The castle itself has eight, four with narrow sentinel towers reaching even higher into the sky.

The town wall was needed here to protect the English settlers trying to take control of the north of Wales, having won a significant battle against the Welsh princes earlier in 1283.

The combination of sea, towers and mountains makes this one of Wales' most attractive castles.

WALK DETAILS

START/FINISH
Conwy railway station, LL32 8LD

DISTANCE
8km (5 miles)

PARKING
Small car park at start, car parks in Conwy

PUBLIC TRANSPORT
Train to Conwy

REFRESHMENTS
Pubs and cafés in Conwy

TOILETS
In castle car park and tourist information centre

THE WALK
Follow in the footsteps of the Anglo-Norman invaders as you walk along the ancient town walls, along the bay and up a hill with incredible views over the sea, castle and surrounding mountains. This walk has some

LEFT Five of the castle's eight towers.

challenging ascents and one slightly tricky descent. Some parts of the route are stony underfoot.

1 From the railway station, head past the Erskine Arms on your left to the town wall ahead. Climb the steps in the tower and follow the wall to the castle.

2 From the modern entrance to the castle, walk straight ahead then right to exit the car park. At the road, turn right downhill. Where the road bends right, cross and turn right towards the castle, then left through an arch to the estuary. Turn left along the quay. At the end, continue through the town wall and follow the road briefly as it bends to the left. Almost immediately, head between two houses – Glan Yr Afon and Shore Cottage – down to the shore. Follow this path around a woodland to a large sign for Bodlondeb Woods on the left, just before a school on the left and footbridge on the right.

3 Turn left into the woods and keep right, skirting the school grounds. At the end of the woods, there are a few steps down onto a tarmac path. Turn

BELOW The castle and town as seen from the ridge near Point 4.

right onto this path, then left onto the road at the end. Cross the A547, then the railway footbridge ahead.

After the bridge, follow the path and then lane along the edge of some woods on the right. At a junction with a residential street (Mountain Road), turn right uphill. Fork right by some parking spaces on the left, signposted Wales Coast Path. Cross the stile and follow the footpath through the woods uphill.

ABOVE The view from between Points 4 and 5.

As the path rises, look behind for an impressive view of the castle.

At a junction of paths, turn right uphill for a fabulous view over Great Orme and Conwy Bay in one direction and Snowdonia in the other.

4 Turn left to follow the path along the ridge with the sea to your right

CASTELL CONWY ■ *CONWY CASTLE*

for just over 1km (⅔ mile), until you start to descend towards a farmhouse with a couple of fields in front.

> There is a good view over Anglesey to your right and, on a clear day, to the right of that you can just see the Isle of Man.

The path bends to the left so the farmhouse is over to the right. At a fork in the path, bear right towards the farmhouse. From here look left and you will be able to see the boundary wall you are heading for. Take care with your footing on this steep section downhill to a junction of paths at the bottom. Head left and find your way to the wall.

5 Turn left on the near side of the wall and follow this path back to the top of Mountain Road, following the boundary wall.

6 Retrace your steps down Mountain Road for a short distance, then follow the road to the right. At the end of Mountain Road, turn left and follow this road to the right until you reach a road bridge over the railway.

Cross the railway here and turn right on the far side of the bridge to find the town wall again. Go under the arch and turn left along the far side of the wall to find the steps up. At the top of the steps, turn left and follow the wall all the way back to the railway station, via the watchtower at the highest point of the town. Alternatively, take a short detour at the top of the steps by continuing straight ahead down to the far end of the wall at the water's edge. There are some wonderful views of the castle along this stretch of the walls.

ABOVE The town wall extending to the water's edge.

BELOW The castle and town from across the river.

CASTELL CONWY ■ *CONWY CASTLE*

18 CASTELL CYDWELI
KIDWELLY CASTLE

Following the Battle of Hastings in 1066, England quickly fell to the Normans. The same cannot be said for Wales, where there was ferocious resistance to the invasion for two centuries before the Welsh were finally defeated.

The Normans constructed a string of castles along the south of Wales but soon found that these castles were vulnerable to attack by Welsh armies. Around 1100, the Normans reasserted control over South Wales, building a second wave of castles to fill some of the gaps along the border and reduce the isolation of those previously built.

Kidwelly was constructed during this second wave. Perched on a steep slope above the River Gwendraeth and defended by a ringwork (a ditch that may have been filled with water) on the more vulnerable side, it was built to be unassailable. However, as with many castles, the defences were not fully effective, and it changed hands several times.

The castle defence was originally an earthen bank, probably with timber palisades and possibly some stonework. Work on the stone castle we see today started in the late 13th century, as the nature of warfare changed and timber became less effective against attack.

WALK DETAILS

START/FINISH
Kidwelly Quay car park, SA17 5EF

DISTANCE
8km (5 miles)

PARKING
At start, car park off Station Road near the town centre

PUBLIC TRANSPORT
Train to Kidwelly (between Points 1 & 2)

REFRESHMENTS
Pubs and cafés in Kidwelly, café at castle (after entry gate), café at Point 3

TOILETS
In Kidwelly SA17 4UU, at farm shop at Point 3

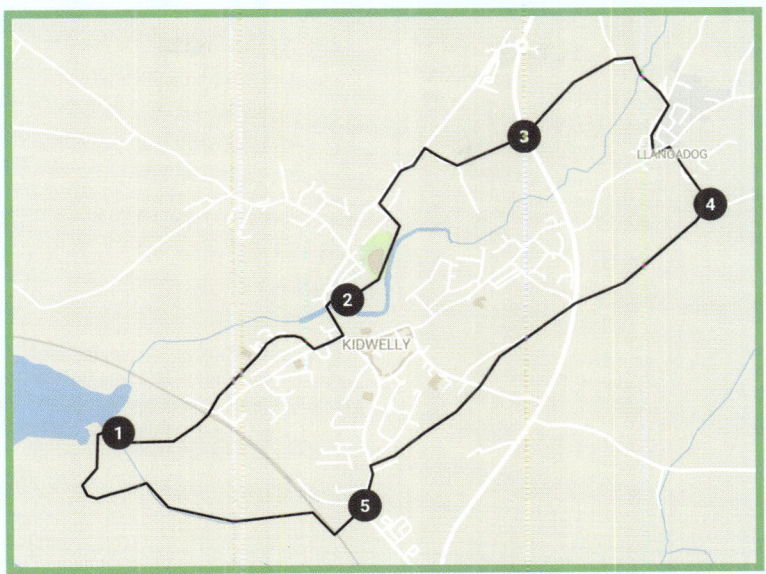

THE WALK

This is a gentle walk with little ascent on easy paths that follow the line of the pretty Gwendraeth valley. It passes between the castle and the river, giving a spectacular view of the fortification, and starts and finishes on the estuary with far-reaching views across the bay.

BELOW The castle from the bank of the ringwork.

1 From Kidwelly Quay, walk back through the car park along the approach road, over the level crossing (join here if arriving by train) and straight ahead on Highfield Villas. This road passes a community centre, fire station and school on the left and bends to the right before meeting Station Road. Turn left onto Station Road, then left again along the main road through Kidwelly. After crossing the river, turn right onto the riverside path and follow this until you reach a mill building on the right.

2 To visit the castle, turn left here then right through the gatehouse. To continue on the walk, head straight on past the mill. After a while, the path runs along the river again, with the castle high on the left. Follow the path as it bends around the castle and rises.

(For a short detour, turn left just before the end of the path and cross to the far corner of the field, followed by the ditch. You are now on the ringworks, with great views of the north and west sides of the castle.)

At the end of the path, go straight ahead to Water Street. Head right for about 300m (330yds), then right again down a small tarmac lane, between a high wall and a hedge bank. Where this lane bends to the right, take the footpath to the left, between hedges, and follow it until you reach an A-road.

3 Cross the road to join a similar path between hedges. Where this path meets a lane, continue in the same direction past Broadford Farm. Cross two streams and continue to the T-junction. Turn right here, behind the houses.

Look ahead and to the right for a distant view of the castle.

At the next T-junction, turn left. Take the first lane on the right, marked with a cul-de-sac sign. After a few metres, fork right past some houses then back into the countryside to a crossroads formed by three tracks and a bridleway.

4 Turn right here onto a lane that passes a couple of houses then becomes a lovely path through woods. At the end of this path, pass through the gates to reach the A-road. On the far side, head through the gates, not the bollards, along another track. As you approach a house, fork left onto a path and follow this to a road. Turn left onto the road, then right immediately after crossing the redundant railway line, signposted Wales Coast Path.

5 Keep the farm buildings close on your left, then follow the track until it rises over the operational

BELOW St Mary's church spire across the river.

railway. Cross the railway, then take an immediate right down a few steps and along the side of a field, following the Wales Coast Path sign. Go through the gate ahead, then along the canal in front. The path on the right is surfaced with gravel; on the left it is grassy. They both end up in the same place.

> This canal was built to transport coal to Kidwelly Quay, and was the first to be built in Wales.

At a substantial junction of paths where a stone bridge crosses the canal, turn left to follow the path

ABOVE The path along the River Gwendraeth.
BELOW The castle rising above the river.

away from the canal.

> On the left is an area of salt marsh (sometimes underwater), a valuable habitat and carbon sink. Across the water is Pembrey Sands Air Weapons Range with its black and yellow air traffic control tower.

Continue on this path until you reach Kidwelly Quay and the car park.

19 CASTELL DINAS BRÂN

The dramatic ruins of the 'Crow's City' dominate the surrounding landscape despite only standing complete for 25 years. This area, squeezed between the expanding Welsh principality of Gwynedd and the invading Anglo-Normans, was ruled by the princes of Powys Fadog. Prince Gruffudd ap Madog was married to an English lady, Emma Audley, so his allegiance was split between England and Wales. In response, Prince Llywelyn of Gwynedd invaded, and Gruffudd lived in exile until deciding to ally himself with Llywelyn. At that point, Gruffudd returned to his land and built Dinas Brân castle in the 1260s.

The approach to the castle was steep on all sides and made more difficult when a dry moat was dug. The stones removed from the moat were used to construct the castle. Gruffudd died shortly after building work was completed. It is thought that the castle was shared equally by his four sons. When the war broke out in 1276, two of the sons supported the Welsh and two the English. The

WALK DETAILS

START/FINISH
Llangollen railway station, LL20 8SN

DISTANCE
9.5km (6 miles)

PARKING
Car parks in Llangollen

PUBLIC TRANSPORT
Train to Llangollen

REFRESHMENTS
Café at Llangollen Wharf, pubs and cafés in Llangollen

TOILETS
At railway station, Llangollen Wharf

BELOW Part of the castle ruins.

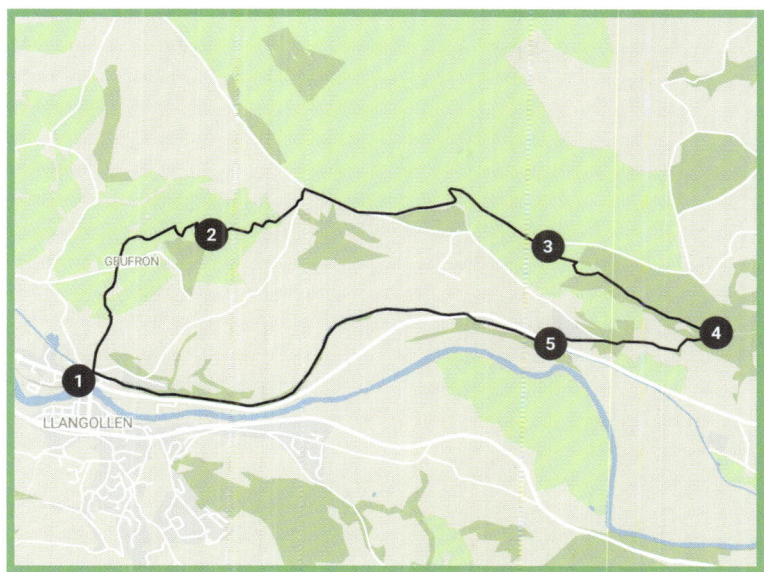

Welsh residents burnt the castle and left it derelict. The English then claimed it but left once they had won the war. After the war, the castle was granted to John de Warenne, who left it abandoned.

The Walk

Set off on the most spectacular canal route, which once transported limestone, slate and iron ore. The path then ascends to the lofty heights of the castle. Walking high along the base of Eglwyseg, views stretch towards England and North Wales. Descend through ancient woodlands for a pleasant final canal-side stroll.

BELOW The castle ruins dominate the landscape.

CASTELL DINAS BRÂN ■ *DINAS BRÂN CASTLE*

1 From the railway station, head uphill away from the river to Llangollen Wharf on the canal. Cross the canal and head straight over the road junction, continuing uphill. You will soon see the castle ahead.

Looking back down over Llangollen, a white tent-like structure dominates the townscape. This is the building that houses the annual International Musical Eisteddfod. The festival has been running since 1947, when it was set up to heal some of the rifts caused by WWII and promote international peace. In the 1990s, a decision was taken to build a permanent structure to house the festival, rather than erecting tents each year, and the design was chosen to reflect those earlier tents. Performers from over 140 countries have taken part in the Eisteddfod, including stars such as Luciano Pavarotti, Margot Fonteyn, Michael Ball and Elaine Paige.

ABOVE The canal towpath between Point 5 and the end.

RIGHT The path leading down from the castle.

Continue uphill on a clear footpath to Pear Tree Cottage, and then again on a stone track. At a crossroads of tracks, continue uphill straight ahead to a gate with a large castle sign. Head diagonally right uphill to the castle.

The hill on which the castle is built is made from shale and siltstone. The quarry from which the castle stone was taken forms a defensive ditch around the site. To the north-east is a limestone scarp slope. Historically, this has been quarried for lime to use in building, mortar, paint or agriculture, but it is now considered to be of national importance and thus protected.

2 Leave the castle by the wood and stone steps, heading towards the mouth of the valley.

Look along the valley for a view of the Pontcysyllte aqueduct. As you walk down the slope, there are some flat areas that may have been hut platforms when this was an Iron Age hill fort.

As you leave the ringworks, follow the path to the left then down through an iron gate to another lane. Turn left, then right at the T-junction. Continue along this lane, past a turning off to the right, along a straight stretch, and around a bend to the left, and then the right. At the end of the next straight stretch, look for a picnic bench on your right and the stone track signposted Offa's Dyke Path to Trefor.

3 Take this track down into the valley. When you reach a gate across the track, turn right down a narrower footpath. At the end of the wall, turn left through a gate below a house. After about 900m (½ mile), you will pass a house a little below the track, and then reach a junction of paths.

4 Turn sharp right downhill. Follow this path through the woods, along the edge of a field and over a stile. Turn left down the drive. At the first steep turn to the left, continue straight ahead on a footpath. Pass through a narrow gate, and after a few metres, take the left fork slightly downhill. When you reach a minor road, take the left route down the hill.

As the road drops, the castle comes back into view ahead.

This road descends to the Sun Trevor pub and a bridge over the canal.

The Llangollen Canal was built to provide a source of water to other canals. After canals were replaced by railways as a means of transportation, the water was used by industry instead. This secured the future of the canal.

5 Cross the canal and turn right along the towpath to return to Llangollen Wharf and the end of the walk.

20 CASTELL DINEFWR

Castell Dinefwr has had a turbulent history. It was owned by a Welsh prince, The Lord Rhys. While the Normans were exerting their rule over the English, The Lord Rhys was establishing himself as a prominent prince in Wales. For the last few years of Rhys' life, he was plagued by disloyal sons trying to usurp him and seize the castle. They were unsuccessful, but on his death, his sons and grandsons continued to fight, brutally transferring ownership of the castle around the family.

In the meantime, Llewelyn the Great was expanding his power base in Gwynedd to the north. In 1220, he forced Rhys' son to demolish some of the castle, although it was not long before it was rebuilt. When Edward I decided it was time to extend his reign over Wales as well as England, the new Lord Rhys handed the castle over to the English forces, who used it as a base while fighting the Welsh defenders. Rhys revolted against the crown and briefly managed to regain it a few years later, but he was ultimately unsuccessful and paid with his life. The castle saw two

WALK DETAILS

START/FINISH
Newton House National Trust car park, Llandeilo SA19 6RT

DISTANCE
7.5km (4¾ miles)

PARKING
At start, in Llandeilo

PUBLIC TRANSPORT
Train to Llandeilo (join walk between Points 7 & 8)

REFRESHMENTS
Pubs and cafés in Llandeilo, café at Newton House

TOILETS
At Newton House, in Llandeilo town centre

BELOW Castell Dinefwr (credit: Crown copyright (2023) Cymru Wales).

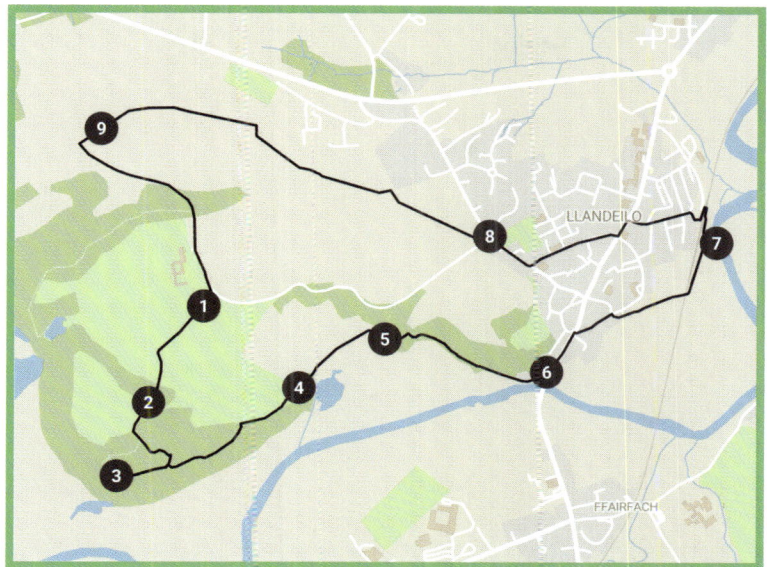

more significant periods of action in the next 200 years. The castle was eventually abandoned when the family moved to the site of what is now Newton House.

THE WALK

A gentle walk across parkland and up through a woodland nature reserve takes you to the castle, which has long views down the river valley. The route undulates to Llandeilo and down to the river before returning through the town and back across the parkland, with great views of Newton House.

1 From the car park, walk south-west past the overflow parking. Follow this track past the wall, downhill, through some trees and then through a gate.

2 At this point, the track bends to the right. To stay on the route, follow the path ahead uphill.

Continue through the walkers' gate and along the clear route through the woods. At the top of the path, turn right to visit the castle.

These days, the castle is obscured by trees until you're almost at the entrance. In its heyday, this whole area would have been clear of vegetation to allow those defending the castle to spot any enemies as they approached.

3 Leave the castle on the same path. Follow the track through the woods and then along the side of the parkland. Shortly before the track bends to the left, fork right on a clear path towards the trees to a walkers' gate.

4 Pass through the gate into the woods. At another walkers' gate, exit the woods. Look ahead and to the right for the next gate. Take this and follow the path along the bottom of the field. After a while, a church will come into view ahead. Continue to the church wall, then turn right through a walkers' gate and follow the path around and into the churchyard.

CASTELL DINEFWR ■ DINEFWR CASTLE

5 **Exit between stone gateposts on the far side of the churchyard.** Follow this path uphill to meet a track. Turn right and follow this track through the woods to the road.

6 **Turn left in front of the line of painted houses and follow the road until you reach the church.** Turn right along Church Street, in front of more painted houses. At the end of the graveyard, turn right down a track between buildings. Follow this track down the hill and under the railway line. Turn left onto the footpath between a fence and railings. The route turns left immediately before the suspension bridge.

LEFT Llandyfeisant Church at Point 5.

BELOW The river from the bridge close to Point 6.

BELOW RIGHT Llandeilo's painted houses from the far side of the river.

Take a short detour onto the bridge for a lovely view of the river, then retrace your steps to return to the same side as earlier.

7 **Follow the path until it reaches the railway station.** Cross using the pedestrian crossing, then turn back on yourself to leave the station via the steps. Turn uphill onto Clarendon Road, then left when you reach the main road. Take the first right, signposted Dinefwr Park, and follow this road for 540m (1/3 mile) to the park entrance.

8 **As you enter the park, look ahead for a distant view of the castle before taking the path running diagonally right across the grass.**

Before long, the square turrets of Newton House come into view on the left. Newton House was built in 1660 by Edward Rice, a descendent of The Lord Rhys, although the turrets were not added until later.

Where the path forks, turn right towards the end of the rugby pitch. After a short flight of steps, turn left. After a few metres, fork right, then left at the next fork, across the meadow. On reaching a track, cross it then turn right up the side of another meadow.

From here, there is another view of the castle to the left.

When this path reaches a track, turn left to follow the track for 600m (1/3 mile) until you reach a barn on the left.

9 **At the next field gate across the track ahead, follow the main track as it turns to the left through high stone gateposts.** This track leads to Newton House and the end of the walk.

CASTELL DINEFWR ■ *DINEFWR CASTLE*

21 CASTELL HARLECH

Work started on Castell Harlech in 1283 as part of Edward I's attempt to quell Welsh rebellion against England's conquest. It took just six years to complete the construction. The castle stands in a prominent position, perched on a steep outcrop of rock and visible for miles. Additionally, the castle has concentric rings of defence that made it very difficult to defeat.

Those attacking the castle were clearly aware of this issue, so they mainly focused on besieging the inhabitants. There have been five sieges, only one of which was thwarted. On that occasion, the water gate was used to bring food supplies, enabling the inhabitants to sit out the siege successfully. During the other sieges, for reasons that are not immediately apparent, this approach did not work, and the inhabitants surrendered in preference to starving to death.

In the inner courtyard of the castle, a narrow flight of steps hugs the wall. This staircase was used by soldiers to reach the battlements without disturbing the dignitaries sleeping in the gatehouse.

After playing its role as the last Royalist stronghold in the British Civil Wars of the 1640s, the castle was partially demolished and left to deteriorate until it was restored in the 20th century.

WALK DETAILS

START/FINISH
Bron y Graig Isaf car park, Harlech LL46 2SR

DISTANCE
7km (4⅓ miles)

PARKING
At start, short- and long-stay parking in Harlech

PUBLIC TRANSPORT
Train to Harlech (join walk at Point 6)

REFRESHMENTS
Pub and cafés in Harlech, café in castle (before entry gate)

TOILETS
In castle and at start

BELOW The castle as seen from between Points 5 and 6.

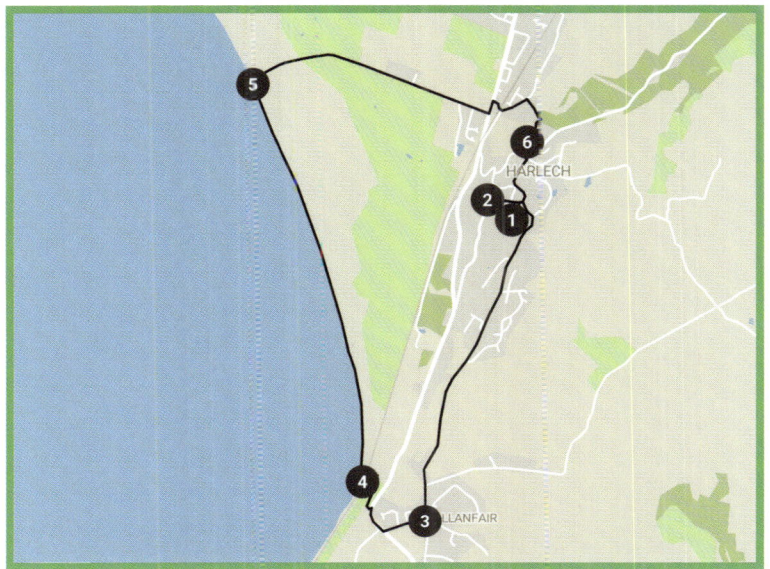

THE WALK

This walk provides stunning views of the castle, the bay and the surrounding landscape. On the far side of the bay, the hills of the Llŷn Peninsula rise gently up into the mountains of Snowdonia inland. A short section may not be passable during very high tides.

1 From the car park, head downhill and turn left along High Street. Follow the pavement into the park on the right, then turn right again after a few metres for a fantastic view of the castle on its rocky promontory.

2 Retrace your steps to the car park. Take the next road right (Bron Y Graig) and follow it around to the right, uphill. At the end of the road, turn left and follow this road for about 2km (1¼ miles).

Before long, you will see far-reaching views over the Tremadog Bay to your right. The bay forms part of a Special Conservation Area. Its sandbanks, rocks, as well as sandy and muddy sediments provide habitats for an abundance of diverse wildlife.

When you reach some houses, look for the next road on the right.

3 Turn towards the A496 past a letterbox and bus stop. The sea is now directly ahead. Turn right onto the A-road then left through a gate opposite Murmur-Y-Don, onto National Trust land Allt-Y-Mor. Follow the clear path to a gate in the far right-hand corner. You are now on the Wales Coast Path.

The Wales Coast Path runs along the entire length of the Welsh coast and was officially opened in May 2012. It is 1,400km long (870 miles) and links with the England Coast Path at each end. It also links up with Offa's Dyke Path, which more or less follows the border with England, meaning you can walk all the way around Wales, if you wish.

Follow this path downhill, over the railway and onto the beach.

4 **Turn right along the beach for 2km (1¼ miles).**

The mountains of Eryri National Park (Snowdonia) are ahead. Eryri is Wales's largest national park, and where the Welsh held out for longest against the Norman invasion, from the 11th to 13th centuries. Over half of Eryri's population speaks Welsh – it is not unusual to hear families chatting and people greeting each other in Welsh around here. Maybe it's time to practise a few words, such as good morning – bore da (said 'borreh dah') and thank you – diolch (said 'deeolch', with a soft L and the 'ch' as in 'loch').

A tall post marks the route taking you off the beach.

Sand dunes are rich in biodiversity. The natural movement of the sand provides a home to a specialised range of plants and animals that have developed to thrive in these conditions. They also help to protect our coastline from erosion, which will become increasingly important with the progression of climate breakdown. And, of course, they provide a gorgeous backdrop to a walk along a beach!

5 **As you leave the dunes, you will see the castle some distance inland.**

Since the 1300s, the bay in front of the castle has silted up; when the castle was built, it had direct access to the water through a sea gate at the bottom of the rocks.

When you reach the gate to the road, head towards the castle along the road. At the end, turn left down the side of the Queens Hotel, and then right to the railway station.

Cross the track using the bridge, walk back down the platform and exit the station. Turn left along the road, and then take the next right opposite Tan-Y-Castell Workshops. This is Ffordd Pen Llech, claimed to be the world's

ABOVE The castle from the park at Point 2.
RIGHT A throne in the park at Point 2.
BELOW Tremadog Bay and the beach followed between Points 4 and 5.

steepest street (a title it did hold for a while), and you are about to find out why!
Continue to the top.

Turn right down Twtil to visit the castle.

6 The route continues straight ahead along Stryd Fawr to return to the start.

22 CASTELL LLANSTEFFAN

The promontory at Llansteffan has long been used as a defensive position. An Iron Age fort was here in 600 BC, and when the Normans arrived around AD 1100, they built their own ringworks on the same site, topped with a timber palisade. Over time, as timber became less effective at repelling attackers, the ringworks were replaced with a stone castle. The imposing gatehouse was built around 1280.

The castle saw a lot of action; understandably, the local Welsh people were not too happy about the Norman invasion, and the castle changed hands on several occasions over the next 300 years.

Towards the end of the 14th century, Henry VII gifted the castle to his uncle, Jasper Tudor. He extended the gatehouse living quarters, moving the gateway to one side of the original position.

Castell Llansteffan is most notable now for its stunning views across the Tywi estuary and Carmarthen Bay. Looking south, the sand has a golden glow and the water sparkles when the sun shines. The River Tywi used to be an important trade route in Roman times, with ships taking wares up to Carmarthen, known then as 'Moridunum', which means 'sea fort'. It's hard to imagine the river that busy now.

WALK DETAILS

START/FINISH
Llansteffan Castle car park, SA33 5JT (follow signs to parking, not the castle)

DISTANCE
8km (5 miles)

PARKING
At start

PUBLIC TRANSPORT
Bus from Carmarthen to church (join at Point 4, Castle Inn). In summer, it may be possible to catch a train to Ferryside and a ferry from there

REFRESHMENTS
Café at start, pubs in Llansteffan

TOILETS
At start

RIGHT Decoration at St Anthony's Well.
BELOW The castle as seen from the road from the village.

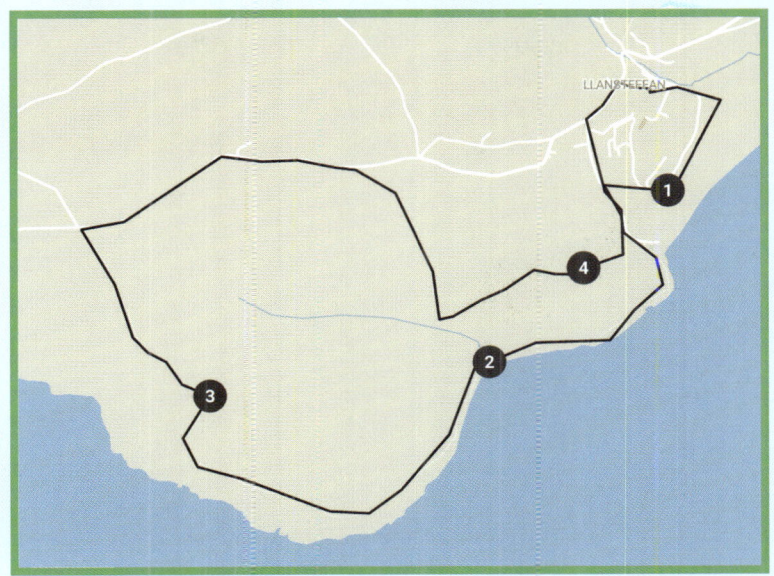

THE WALK

The first leg of this walk follows the coastline, with views over Carmarthen Bay. The return leg travels back to the castle and village via quiet lanes that run through the rolling Carmarthenshire hills. The path can get muddy in places. A fair amount of ascent and descent.

1 From the car park, turn right onto the beach if the tide is out. Walk along the base of the cliffs around the headland and up the

stone ramp to join the path at St Anthony's Cottage. If the tide is in or coming in, head up on the tarmac path signposted to the castle and Wales Coast Path. At the top of the path, turn left onto the lane and head towards the castle. Fork right at the junction, then turn left into the woods following the Wales Coast Path sign.

> The ornate bench on your right commemorates the mock mayor-making, concerts and cultural events that took place here during Miners' Fortnight.

At the shelter, you can either take the steps down to the beach or remain on the path as it turns to the right and continues to St Anthony's Cottage. Immediately before crossing the stream, turn uphill for about 30m (100ft) if you would like to visit St Anthony's Well, an ancient pilgrimage site. Look for a gate in a stone archway with a sign that says 'Ffynnon Antwn Sant'.

2 Back on the coast path, pass through a white gate and cross the stream. Continue in front of St Anthony's house, through another white gate, and straight ahead past a cottage. The next section of path travels through what is known as a Celtic rainforest because of its diverse flora and fauna.

ABOVE The Twyi Estuary.

BELOW The castle and village from the far side of the Twyi.

CASTELL LLANSTEFFAN ■ *LLANSTEFFAN CASTLE*

Conditions here are warmer than average, with more light due to reflection from the sea. This means that you might see maidenhair ferns, sea spleenwort and rare centipedes.

This section of path can get muddy. Continue along the coast path for 1.5km (1 mile) where the path turns inland and meets a lane.

3 Turn left onto the lane. At the next T-junction, leave the Wales Coast Path and turn right. Follow this lane for just over 1km (⅔ mile). Close to the brow of a hill, look out for a kissing gate and a battered footpath sign on the left. Turn your back to those, and take the kissing gate 10m (33ft) down the track ahead. Follow the footpath, with the hedge to your right. Pass through a gate and continue with the hedge on your right, with a view of the castle to your left. About halfway down the field, hidden behind a tree, take the kissing gate on the right and walk down the field, now with the hedge on your left, towards a house. The next kissing gate you need is between the house and garage. Pass through this and walk in front of the house down the drive. At a junction of drives, keep left. This will eventually take you around to the entrance of the castle – you will see a sign just past Castle Hill Cottage.

4 Continue on the drive to return to the top of the tarmac path from the car park, and walk past it to visit the village itself.

Layers of history are evident in the church. The original medieval font is inside, parts were built in the 13th and 15th centuries, and the Victorians refurbished the interior in the 19th century.

Turn right in front of the Castle Inn pub. Pass the shop, then take the next residential street on the right – Maes Griffith. The footpath runs down the side and rear of gardens to a road. Cross and keep the playing field fence on your right. Walk straight through the car park ahead and turn right along the edge of the beach, back to the start.

CASTELL LLANSTEFFAN ■ *LLANSTEFFAN CASTLE*

23 CASTELL POWIS

Although Powis was one of the three major Welsh principalities, it has often found itself between a rock and a hard place. There have been periods of rule from Gwynedd to the north, as well as overlordship from England to the east.

Relationships were not always harmonious within the family, either. In 1309, Hawise inherited the estate. Her uncles disputed her claim and besieged the castle. The castle and its mistress survived, and her claim was confirmed by royal charter. However, one of her uncles did not give up and continued to periodically attack the castle.

In 1400, the castle was held for the king against assault by Owain Glyndŵr.

The final hurrah of the castle came in 1644 during the British Civil Wars. Parliamentary troops blew up the outer gate and successfully entered. Luckily for us, they did not fulfil their orders to level the entire castle. Instead, they chose to destroy only the outer defences.

WALK DETAILS

START/FINISH
Welshpool railway station, SY21 7AZ

DISTANCE
7km (4⅓ miles)

PARKING
At start or at the castle, car parks in Welshpool

PUBLIC TRANSPORT
Train or bus to Welshpool railway station

REFRESHMENTS
Pubs and cafés in Welshpool, café in castle (after entry gate)

TOILETS
In castle (before entry gate), Welshpool Tourist Information Centre

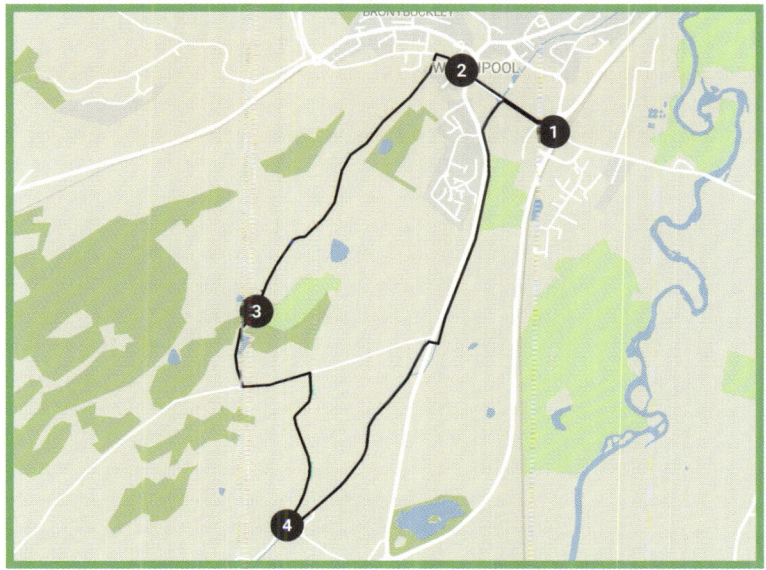

In 1801, the castle was inherited and later refurbished by Edward Clive, son of Clive of India. The castle houses the Clive Collection, which includes many spoils of war from the conquest of India, as well as diplomatic gifts and trinkets from the family's travels.

LEFT The castle from the gardens (credit: Crown copyright (2023) Cymru Wales).

BELOW A memorial to the steam railway.

THE WALK

An easy walk through delightful countryside encompassing the castle, a section of the Montgomery Canal and a Georgian market town. Dogs cannot be taken on this walk, as it passes through a privately owned deer park. There is a short section across a field. The rest is all on tarmac and gravel paths.

1 Take the road into the town centre, passing the Old Station on the left and a stone circle on the right.

Stone circles like these can be found all over Wales – they are Gorsedd Stones, used during the National Eisteddfod. Each has a flat stone at the centre of the circle, used as a platform for ceremonies during the festival. The National Eisteddfod is an annual celebration of Welsh culture and language.

The Georgian houses on the right are typical of Welshpool.

Cross the canal and continue into the town centre.

2 Shortly after the market hall on the right (also the town hall), turn left signposted Castell Powis. Pass through the gate into Castle Parks and follow the drive towards the castle. You will get tantalising glimpses of it as you rise up the hill. Take the right fork towards the car park and ticket office, with the castle now on a rise to your left.

3 After visiting the castle, continue in the same direction along the drive, past a lily pond on the left and back into parkland. Take the pedestrian gate to the side of the cattle grid. At the entrance to Castle Parks, the pedestrian gate is on the right side of the main gate, at the end of the wall. Turn left onto the road. In 350m (⅕ mile), where another road joins from the left, take the footpath on the right across a field. Look to the right to see the bridge that you need to cross in the bottom of the valley. After crossing the bridge, head through the gate and follow the fence over the rise and around to the right. Through the gate ahead, you can see the canal to the left. The route follows the old track, which is now a grassy ledge with the remnants of a hedge each side of it. This heads diagonally downhill to the water.

This is the Montgomery Canal, built in 1797. Lime and coal were transported along the canal to kilns, where the lime was heated to create quicklime, a fertiliser that was spread on canal-side fields. Within 100 years, the canal was struggling as the agricultural sector was depressed and other forms of

BELOW The castle from the park between Points 2 and 3.

ABOVE The Montgomery Canal between Point 4 and Welshpool.

fertiliser were introduced. It staggered on until 1944, when there was a big leak that was not worth repairing. Over the last 30 years or so, it has been restored and become a valuable resource for recreation and wildlife, including otters.

4 Cross the canal and turn right to cross back under the bridge. Follow the towpath back to Welshpool, with the canal on your left.

This section of canal is not used by boats, so the water is clear and festooned in places with waterlilies and other plants.

In Welshpool, pass the supermarket and wharf (now a museum) on the left before rising to the road that crosses at bridge 119. Turn right, heading back back to the station.

Welshpool was initially known as 'Pool'. 'Welsh' was added to the beginning to avoid confusion with the English town 'Poole'.

Welshpool is home to a narrow-gauge railway, as well as being on the main rail network. Trains used to weave their way through the town to the networked station. The line always struggled financially, but managed to survive from 1901 to 1956. In the early 60s, a band of dedicated locals set about preserving the railway, and thanks to their labour of love, trains are running on the line again. However, it is no longer possible to run trains through the town centre, so the terminus is on the far side of town.

24 CASTELL Y WAUN
CHIRK CASTLE

Edward I gave Roger Mortimer the Welsh Chirklands to thank him for his service in defeating the Welsh in 1282. Under royal licence, he began to build this defensive castle in 1295.

Britain was in a period of political instability, with battles raging as powerful men tried to wrest control from each other. For the next three centuries, ownership of the castle passed between powerful magnates, until Thomas Myddelton bought it in 1595. His family then owned it for almost 400 years before it was acquired first by the state and then the National Trust in the late 20th century.

Thomas Myddelton was a wealthy entrepreneur who was one of the founders of the East India Company. So, much of the family's prosperity was derived from human exploitation.

During the British Civil Wars, the castle was besieged and taken by Royalists. Later, back in the hands of the Myddeltons, the castle was attacked by Parliamentarians, who had orders to destroy it. It was damaged but not totally destroyed.

During the 20th century, life in the castle was somewhat different. Lord Howard de Walden leased it for almost 50 years. He re-roofed and re-glazed it, introduced central heating and installed flushing toilets. His guests were many and influential, ranging from notable politicians to theatrical creatives.

WALK DETAILS

START/FINISH
Caffi Wylfa car park, Chirk LL14 5BS

DISTANCE
11.25km (7 miles)

PARKING
At start, castle or town centre

PUBLIC TRANSPORT
Train to Chirk, coach from London to Chirk railway station

REFRESHMENTS
Cafés at start and in castle, pubs and cafés in Chirk, pub at Chirk Bank

TOILETS
In town centre

BELOW The castle from its gardens (credit: Renee Denise/Shutterstock).

THE WALK

Meander through a dark canal tunnel, under a lofty aqueduct, across parkland and, of course, to the castle with its wonderful topiary and gardens. This walk has fabulous views, reached via some steep climbs, muddy ground and several stiles. Do not attempt when the river is flooded (the valley is visible from the canal near the start).

1 From the car park, turn right onto the road. Just before the mini roundabout, turn left down the tarmac path. At the bottom, turn right onto the towpath and into the tunnel. The path is flat and there's a handrail, but it gets very dark, so you might want to light the way.

BELOW Entering the tunnel.

CASTELL Y WAUN ■ *CHIRK CASTLE*

(If you would prefer to stay above ground, take a right at the mini roundabout, turning left at the next junction to rejoin the route at the far end of the tunnel at Point 2.)

After emerging, take the first path on the right leading up to the top of the tunnel.

2 Turn right along the parapet before reaching the road. At the top of the slope, take the path to the right. Keep the field visible on your left, and after 150m (165yds) turn left through the kissing gate. Cross the field, following the power lines. At the far side, turn left onto the lane for a short detour to see the castle gates. Otherwise, dogleg right then left, passing between Snowdrop Cottage and another house to follow a waymarked route to the castle. Follow the drive to the ticket office.

> *There is a view of the castle to the left on the approach to the car park.*

3 After visiting the castle, take the path along the left side of the car park heading north-west. Follow the waymarkers with red arrows, keeping the field boundary on your left, until you reach a lane and Rose Cottage. Head up the road and turn left immediately after the cottages. Follow the path uphill and then down, keeping the fence line some distance to the left.

At the end of the field, take the steps down to a stone track. Turn left along the track and follow it downhill. At 1 Ty Brickley, keep left. A few metres further along, keep right at the junction, heading downhill to the road at the valley bottom.

4 Cross the road into Castle Mill. Cross the river and follow the tarmac road steeply uphill. At the T-junction, take the steps directly ahead. (To avoid a steep climb, turn left onto the road and rejoin the route at Point 5.) At the top, turn right, away from the private drive. Pass through one gate and then turn left to follow the acorn waymarkers up the field, keeping close to the right-hand boundary.

> *Turn around for a view of the castle behind you.*

At the top of the field, cross the stile and turn left along the stony track. When the track meets a tarmac road, head straight over and follow the road downhill. After a short distance, take the well-hidden stile on the left and head straight down the field, passing a garden and house on the right. Take the path to the right of the old schoolhouse. Turn right onto the footpath to the road.

5 Continue ahead for about 175m (190yds). Turn left over a stile into Pentre Wood. Follow the clear path as it leads diagonally down to the river. At the river, turn right through a field and along a road until you reach a bridge. Cross the bridge and continue to follow the river downstream on the other side. Pass under the aqueduct and viaduct and continue to follow the river until a ramp leads up to a road ahead.

6 Pass the Bridge Inn and head up Chirk Bank. Turn right along the canal towpath to cross the aqueduct. Just before the tunnel, bear right up the ramp to the roundabout. Turn right to return to the start.

ABOVE The castle as seen from between Points 4 & 5.

BELOW Chirk Viaduct with the aqueduct behind.

25 CASTLE CAMPBELL

Castle Campbell stands at the head of a steep, densely wooded glen between the deep ravines formed by the rushing waters of the burns of Care and Sorrow. The castle commands superb views all the way to the Queensferry Crossing on the Firth of Forth.

The current tower was built around 1430. At the time, it was called Castle Glume, but when it came into Colin Campbell's ownership later that century, he petitioned the king to change the name, and thus it became Castle Campbell. The Campbells, who were the earls of Argyll, used the castle as their Lowland seat for 200 years until they moved to a townhouse in Stirling.

A host of interesting characters stayed at the castle, including the reformist preacher John Knox, who founded the Presbyterian Church of Scotland, and Mary, Queen of Scots. In the 1590s, the castle was remodelled. An inventory taken at the time indicates that there were 47 beds in the castle – plenty of room for visitors.

WALK DETAILS

START/FINISH
Dollar Community Woodland, Upper Hillfoot Road, Dollar FK14 7PL

DISTANCE
7.5km (4⅔ miles)

PARKING
At start, Point 4 and castle car park on Castle Road

PUBLIC TRANSPORT
Bus from Edinburgh to King's Seat (join walk at Point 5)

REFRESHMENTS
Pubs and cafés in Dollar

TOILETS
None at the time of writing. Some are planned in the village – check Dollar Community Development Trust website for more information

The castle met its fate in response to Oliver Cromwell's army being garrisoned there. Royalists attacked and set fire to it. Following the restoration of the monarchy, Campbell was executed, and the castle was left to decay.

THE WALK
Climb a hill with distant views before descending to Dollar Glen. Breathe oxygen liberated from oak leaves at eye height, perched above drops to fast-flowing waters and plunge pools. Castle Campbell disappears and reappears among the trees before you finally reach it. Winding woodland paths, uneven in places with steep drops.

LEFT The castle from above, with views to the Queensferry Crossing.

BELOW The copse atop Law Hill at Point 2.

1 Take the path on the far side of the car park and turn left at the junction. After crossing the stream, turn left to stay close to the edge of the woodland. Turn left between meadows and follow the path to the stand of trees on the hilltop.

CASTLE CAMPBELL

2 Head straight over the hill and along the ridge to the trig point. Retrace your steps back through the stand of trees and down to the community woodland. At the woodland, turn left and follow the path around the edge. Cross the stream and stay left. Stay on the main track as it bends to the right and ultimately to the woodland entrance. Cross the side road and head left signposted Tillicoultry. Continue to the outskirts of the village.

3 Turn right alongside a house called Rising Hill then behind gardens. When you reach the tarmac lane, Dollar Glen is in front of you. Turn left downhill to a stone-walled entrance to the glen.

4 Turn right through the entrance, onto a footpath heading downhill, all the way to the riverside. Follow the river to a junction of paths with a bench overlooking rapids. Turn left, slightly away from the water. A short distance later, this narrow path rejoins the main path. Turn left. This path leads to a tarmac lane. Turn right. At the T-junction, turn right downhill. At the next T-junction, continue down the hill to the museum.

5 Turn right along the side of the museum. The stream is on your left. Before long, you will reach Mill Green.

Look up for your first peek at the castle just visible above the tree line.

At a junction of paths in the woods, turn left over a footbridge and continue upstream.

ABOVE The castle from the far side of Dollar Glen between Points 5 and 6.

LEFT One of the many cascades on the route.

Close to the top of the path, if you look behind you and slightly to the left, you can see the suspension bridge over the Firth of Forth at Queensferry. As the path begins to drop, look ahead and to the right for a fine view of the castle.

As you near the water, there is a path on the right to a viewpoint. Turn down the path, as the extra 240m (260yds) of descent and ascent is well worth the view at the end.

Return to the path and continue with the burn on your right. Cross the footbridge and climb up on the castle side of the glen. (If you want to shorten the walk, continue up towards the castle.)

6 The route turns left along the line of the stream (the Burn of Sorrow) and crosses it several times before heading along the next gorge. Turn right over the first footbridge and follow the path back down the gorge. Pass through a metal gate, and turn left up onto the knoll for a view over the castle and the countryside to the south. Return to the gate and turn left downhill. The path zigzags down the slope, and when you reach a path along the valley, turn left. This leads to the castle drive. Turn right to visit the castle.

7 Leave the castle by the tarmac drive. About 20m (65ft) after the end of the castle car park, take the narrow footpath on the left up some steps and along a dilapidated stone wall. When the path turns through the wall, turn right, so the wall is now on your right. This narrow path arrives at a track. Turn right and follow the track downhill to the road. Turn right to return to the start.

26 CASTLE STALKER

It is hard to imagine a more romantic setting for a castle: perched on a rock surrounded by water and distant hills. However, the history of Castle Stalker has been far from romantic.

A small fort was built here by the MacDougalls, the Lords of Lorn, around 1320. (See also Dunstaffnage and Dunollie Castles – Walk 34.) By 1390, the lordship and the castle had passed to the Stewarts.

Subsequently, a feud developed between the Stewarts and MacDougalls, leading to bloodshed and loss of life on both sides. A couple of centuries later, the Campbells waded in by murdering Sir Alexander Stewart of Invernahyle in 1520 while he was fishing nearby. A century after that, the Stewarts lost the castle in a drunken wager – to the Campbells. King James VII of Scotland gifted the castle back to the Stewarts, but he was then defeated at the Battle of Dunkeld, and the castle returned to the Campbells.

During the second Jacobite rising of 1745, the Stewarts bombarded the castle with cannon balls. The castle held, and the Campbells remained until 1800, when they left it to decay. A century later, it was bought by the Stewarts and renovated, and it remains in the family today.

THE WALK
The most peaceful start to a walk, through woodland and meadow on a minor road heading to Port Appin. Visit caves and a high limestone arch and cross a boardwalk over a sea inlet with striking views of Castle Stalker set against the mountains of the Highlands.

WALK DETAILS

START/FINISH
Appin Village Hall, PA38 4BG

DISTANCE
13.5km (8⅓ miles)

PARKING
In car park and lay-by opposite start

PUBLIC TRANSPORT
Bus from Fort William to Kirkton (Appin)

REFRESHMENTS
Pubs and café in Port Appin

TOILETS
In Port Appin car park

RIGHT The castle stands on a rocky islet (credit: iStock).

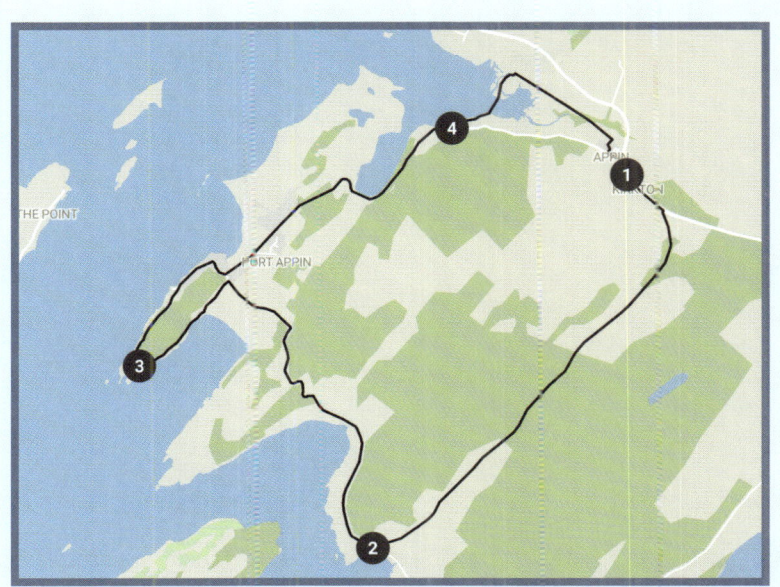

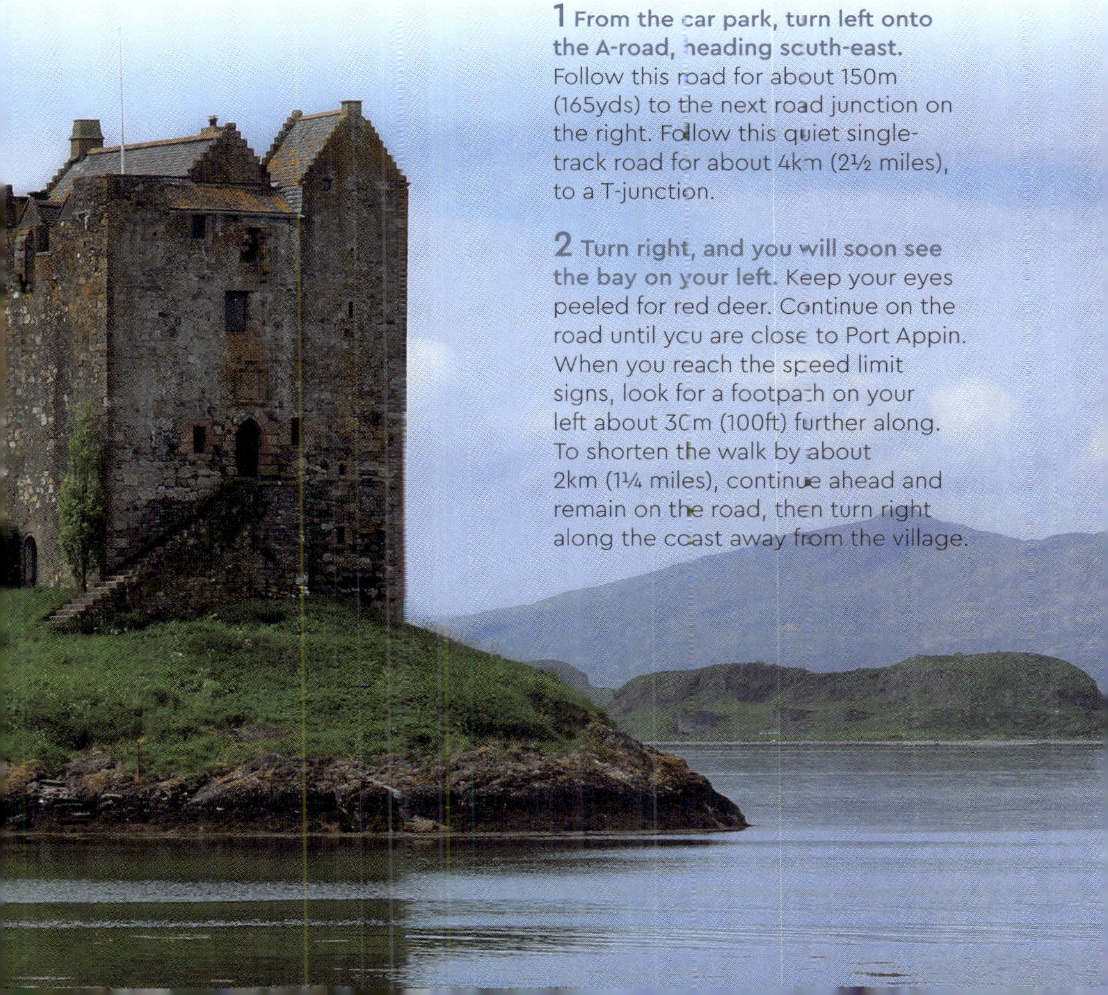

1 From the car park, turn left onto the A-road, heading south-east. Follow this road for about 150m (165yds) to the next road junction on the right. Follow this quiet single-track road for about 4km (2½ miles), to a T-junction.

2 Turn right, and you will soon see the bay on your left. Keep your eyes peeled for red deer. Continue on the road until you are close to Port Appin. When you reach the speed limit signs, look for a footpath on your left about 30m (100ft) further along. To shorten the walk by about 2km (1¼ miles), continue ahead and remain on the road, then turn right along the coast away from the village.

ABOVE Clach Thoull.

Take the road from Port Appin with the sea on your left. You will pass an information board set up inside the old lighthouse lantern section.

> *The new Sgeir Bhuidhe lighthouse is what you can see over the water, and is powered by solar electricity rather than gas. When the old lighthouse was due to be removed, protestors painted it pink with yellow spots and a sad mouth.*

Stay left at the junction, and continue with the sea on your left until you reach Loch Laich and the footpath to Jubilee Bridge.

4 Take the footpath.

> *Castle Stalker is visible on an island to your left.*
>
> *The Jubilee Bridge was first built to celebrate Queen Victoria's Diamond Jubilee in 1887. Before it was built, people crossed the marsh and river at low tide using a waymarked route. A major refurbishment in 1950 involved the creation of a temporary railway line to the bridge to transport materials. In 1986 it was refurbished again, but the tides, salt and winds did not take long to destroy it once more. This century, it has been renovated using materials more suited to the environment and provides walkers, wheelchair users and cyclists access across the salt marsh to join up with the cycle path along the disused railway.*
>
> *You are walking across tidal salt marshes known as 'An Marach'. Salt marshes are wonderful for wildlife. The Eurasian water vole lives here. You are unlikely to see one, but you might hear a plop as one*

This footpath takes you along the edge of a woodland to a house and the shore. Take the track away from the house with the bay to your left.

> *As you near cliffs on your right, look for caves in the cliff wall. A little further on, there's an impressive natural arch with a path underneath. Known as Clach Thoull, it was created by wave erosion when the bottom of the cliffs was at sea level. Since the last Ice Age, the west coast of Scotland has been rising, creating raised beaches. This is what now stands in front of the arch, enabling you to walk through it without getting wet.*

3 Continue along the drive until you reach the village of Port Appin.

> *A small ferry for foot passengers and cycles crosses the Lynn of Lorn to Lismore from the jetty at Port Appin.*

enters the water. You have a better chance of seeing an otter hunting, or a heron standing sentinel over a pool, keeping an eye out for fish. Also look out for ducks, butterflies and dragonflies.

Once you reach the disused railway line that is now part of the National Cycle Network, turn right towards

ABOVE Jubilee Bridge.

BELOW The castle as seen from Jubilee Bridge just after Point 4.

Appin. At the outskirts of Appin, turn right and then left up a residential street. At the top, turn left towards Gunn's Garage. Turn right onto the A-road, and follow it until you reach the end of the walk.

27 CLIFFORD'S TOWER

Only the keep remains of York's largest castle, perched high on its motte, between the rivers Foss and Ouse. Clifford's Tower is uniquely shaped like a four-leaf clover. Lucky for some, but certainly not everyone.

William the Conqueror built the castle in an attempt to control the north of England. York was not the only strategically important place in the country, though, so he and his descendants had a lot of castles to build – for which they needed money. William invited Jews to England to lend him money for his castle-building, as Christians were not permitted to lend money at the time, and Jews were not permitted to do much else.

Towards the end of the 12th century, a wave of anti-Semitism swept through the country and the Jews in York took refuge in the castle. The castle was besieged for so long that they realised they would not survive. Tragically, some took their

WALK DETAILS

START/FINISH
York railway station, YO24 1AB

DISTANCE
9km (5½ miles)

PARKING
Car parks in York

PUBLIC TRANSPORT
Train or coach to York

REFRESHMENTS
Pubs and cafés in York

TOILETS
At start

BELOW Clifford's Tower is reached up a flight of steps.

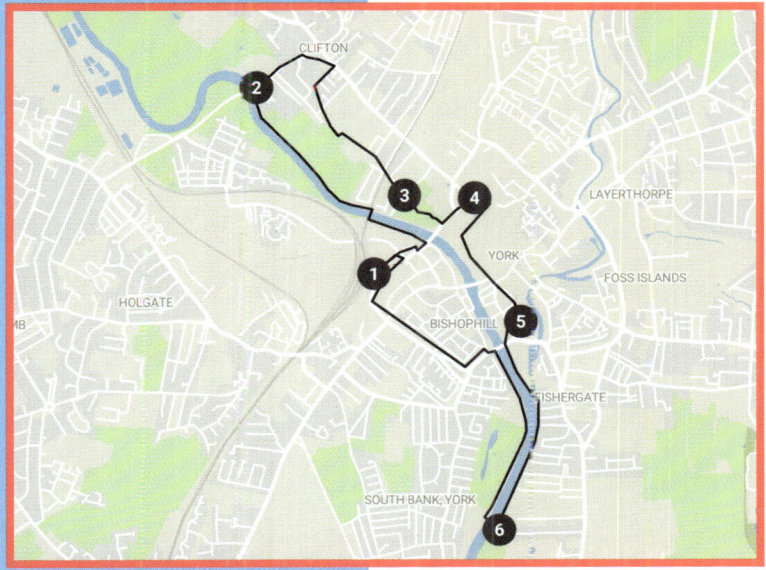

own lives, and the others – having been promised protection – were massacred as they left. It is thought that 150 people lost their lives.

Thankfully, York is a friendlier place today, and visitors of all persuasions enjoy Clifford's Tower and the grand views from its roof deck.

THE WALK

A relaxing stroll by the riverside, along the city walls and through the centre of York provides a delightful introduction to this ancient city. Home to Romans, Saxons, Vikings, and then the Normans, who built many of the landmarks we see today, such as the castle and minster.

1 From the main entrance of the railway station, face the city walls and turn left onto Station Road. Follow it under the old city wall. Turn left, and just before the bridge, turn left again and down a flight of steps. Turn left at the bottom, to walk along the river. Cross the footbridge a few hundred metres ahead, then turn right down some steps to return to the riverbank. Turn right to continue with the river on your left until you reach a road bridge.

2 Turn right. When you reach a triangular green, fork right onto Clifton Green. On the far side of the green, turn right onto Compton Street. At the end, turn left onto a lane, which soon turns into a

CLIFFORD'S TOWER   121

TOP Boats moored on the River Ouse between Point 6 and the end of the walk.

BELOW The ruins of Tower Abbey.

BELOW RIGHT York Minster as seen from the city walls between Point 6 and the end of the walk.

footpath. Continue ahead across several roads, then pass under the railway. Continuing in approximately the same direction, past a car park on your right and along another quiet road – Marygate Lane. Dogleg left then right through the arch ahead into York Museum Gardens.

3 Continue in the same direction, passing the ruins of Tower Abbey on your left and the Hospitium on your right. When the museum is to your left, fork left past York Observatory and continue to the exit. Turn left. This road will take you to York Minster.

> *The first minster was burnt during the unrest following the Norman invasion and rebuilt by the Normans shortly afterwards. What we see today is the result of hundreds of years of building work after that, as well as the restoration work completed after no fewer than four major fires.*

4 Walk between the minster and St Michael Le Belfrey church. At the south entrance to the minster,

CLIFFORD'S TOWER

turn right along Minster Gates, then continue ahead along Stonegate until you reach the end of the road at York Mansion House.

Turn left and continue ahead until you reach a vehicular road and Coppergate. Fork left down Castlegate to Clifford's Tower. The entrance is on the far side of the motte.

5 With your back to the steps, turn right down to the road. Cross into St George's Gardens and turn left at the river. Follow the river until it meets the Foss Navigation, where a footbridge takes you across the canal.

> As you cross the bridge, look to your left for a good view of one of York's flood gates. York sits on the confluence of two major rivers, the Foss and the Ouse. As the land is low-lying, the city has always suffered from a degree of flooding. However, climate breakdown and poor upstream land management practices led to more significant flooding in the early 21st century. Flood gates such as these are part of a larger scheme to protect York from further catastrophic flooding.

Continue with the river on your right to the Millennium Footbridge.

6 Cross the river and turn right to return down the riverside to the city. When you reach a road bridge, pass underneath the bridge then climb up a flight of steps. Turn away from the river and after a few metres, look to your right for the steps up onto the old city walls

> You're about to climb the motte of York's second castle, Old Baile. York was unusual in having two Norman castles. A chain between them helped to control potential invaders using the River Ouse.

The wall walk will eventually lead you to the station. When you see the station on the left, take the first steps down on the right. Turn right under the bridge and then left to return to the station.

CLIFFORD'S TOWER

28 CORFE CASTLE

Corfe Castle is in a stunning location, on a hill in a gap between two ridges. It is an impressive sight despite being a ruin. Imagine what it would have looked like in its heyday, rendered and whitewashed.

Although what we see today is the remains of a Norman castle, there was an earlier castle on this site. In AD 975, King Edward took over the reign of his father, King Edgar. Edgar's second wife, mother to his second son, was not happy about that and ordered Edward's murder – which happened here at Corfe Castle.

The most significant test of the castle's defences came during the British Civil Wars in the 1640s. By this time, the castle had been turned into a stately home owned by the Bankes family. As Royalists, their assets were forfeited. Lady Mary Bankes was having none of it and successfully defended her home with a small army. The siege lasted for six weeks, and the attackers lost 100 men. The defenders lost two. Three years later, the castle was lost during its second siege – because one of Lady Bankes' men opened the sully port and let some Parliamentarians in. The castle was destroyed to avoid any further use of it.

WALK DETAILS

START/FINISH
The Market Cross, Corfe Castle (village) BH20 5EZ

DISTANCE
7.25km (4½ miles)

PARKING
Car parks in Corfe Castle, Norden Park and Ride, car park at Point 2

PUBLIC TRANSPORT
Bus 40 from Wareham to village centre

REFRESHMENTS
Pubs and cafés in village

TOILETS
At castle (before entry gate)

BELOW Corfe Castle sits on a hill in a gap between two ridges.

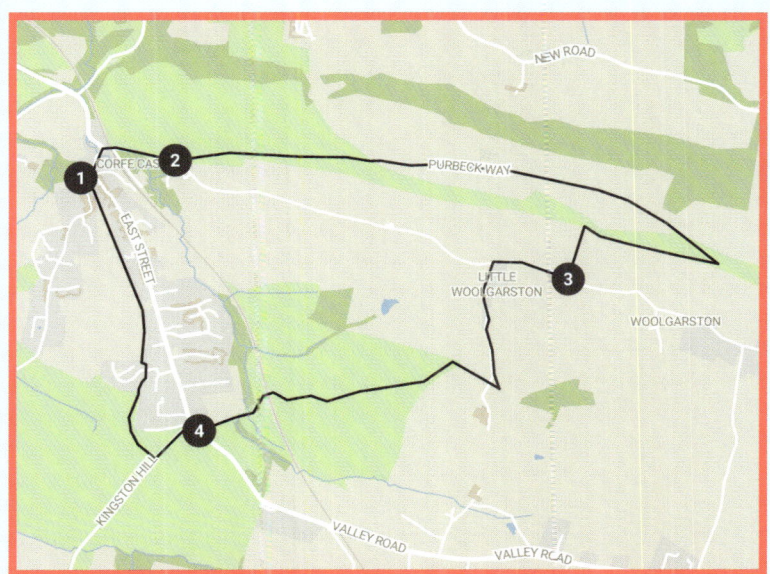

THE WALK

This walk starts in the mellow stone village of Corfe Castle. It heads onto the ridge to the east, with fine views over Poole Harbour. After dropping back down, it crosses Corfe Common, with excellent views of the castle. Much of the route is on bridleways, and horses graze in the fields.

> *The market cross was erected to commemorate Queen Victoria's diamond jubilee in 1897.*

1 From the market cross, head downhill between the Greyhound pub and Bankes Arms hotel. Cross the mill stream, then turn right up Sandy Hill Lane. Follow this road for about 300m (330yds) to Challow walkers' car park.

2 Immediately after the car park, fork left onto a bridle path. After about 200m (220yds), stay left at the stone waymarker and steadily climb onto the ridge.

> *By the time you reach the communications tower, there is an excellent view of the castle behind you.*

From here, continue to head uphill, following the Purbeck Way. Where the fence line moves away to the left and the view opens up over Poole Harbour, fork right on a track downhill. As the track nears a fence, turn sharp right onto a path with the fence on your left. This path has a couple of small sinkholes – please take care. After some time, you will reach the first junction of paths. Turn left through a small gate signposted Woolgarston. This path takes you down the side of paddocks to a small road.

3 Turn right and follow the road for around 300m (330yds). At the first road junction, turn left down a very quiet lane, past a handful of houses. At the end of the tarmac lane, bear right onto a farm drive, and after a few metres, turn right through a gate. Follow the clear path to the top left-hand corner of the field. Pass through the gate at the top. You are now on Corfe Common, owned by the National Trust.

As common land, some locals still have grazing rights, so you might come across horses or cattle grazing here. Because the land has not been ploughed for centuries, it still holds traces of ancient field systems and trackways. The soil is sandstone and clay, and is wet in areas, resulting in diverse flora.

(To shorten the walk, keep the hedge line on your right all the way back into the village.)

To continue on the route, bear left along a faint path as it follows the other hedge line and then bends right across the common. You are heading for the far left-hand edge of the village.

Look to your right for a fabulous view of the castle.

BELOW The track between Points 2 and 3 is a bridleway, open to walkers, horse-riders and cyclists.

This path eventually leads to a stone bridge over the railway line. Cross the bridge and follow the rough stone track the other side until you reach a road.

4 Turn right, then take the first road on the left. This is a B-road, so please take care and face into the oncoming traffic. After about 200m (220yds), the solid white line along the side of the road becomes a dashed line. Turn right here onto the footpath signposted Corfe Castle. Bear right to skirt the left-hand edge of a garden. Keep the gardens on your right and the common on your left until you reach a gate. Head through the gate and along the path beyond, between gardens. At the end of the gardens, continue downhill to a T-junction. Take the path between houses opposite the junction. Turn right through the kissing gate onto another area of open land.

> *This is The Halves, and was once split into blocks and rented to local people for growing crops.*

The castle is ahead. Take the clear path ahead along the right-hand boundary of the field, through another two gates and directly towards the castle. When you reach the children's playground, turn left and follow signs into the village centre to complete the walk.

ABOVE The castle as seen from between Points 2 and 3.

BELOW The view over Poole Harbour from the ridge between Points 2 and 3.

29 DARTMOUTH CASTLE

Dartmouth Castle is in the most wonderful position, right at the mouth of the River Dart. Unusually, it was built by the townspeople rather than a king or wealthy landowner and was never a lordly seat. Only one section of wall and tower remains of the original castle; most of what we see today are more modern updates.

In times past, the townsfolk of Dartmouth made their money partly by privateering – and sometimes crossed the blurry line to piracy. Raids were made on French ports and towns along the coast, and the French often tried to retaliate, which is why Dartmouth needed protection.

A chain was soon hung across the river to stop enemy boats from reaching the harbour. The chain was usually kept in the tower and laid out at river height by joining sections together and resting them on cobles – flat-bottomed boats. The length of the chain was adjusted as the tide rose and fell.

The castle was brought back into use in WWII, and a similar barrier was placed across the river. This time, it was a floating barrage with a net hanging below to ensnare submarines, with mines as a back-up.

LEFT Dartmouth Castle was built to defend river access to the town.

WALK DETAILS

START/FINISH
Little Dartmouth National Trust car park, TQ6 0JR

DISTANCE
7.5km (4⅔ miles)

PARKING
At start, a few spaces at castle

PUBLIC TRANSPORT
Bus from Totnes to Dartmouth

REFRESHMENTS
Café at castle, pubs and cafés in Dartmouth

TOILETS
At castle (before entry gate)

THE WALK

The walk to the castle is mainly along quiet country lanes. Once it reaches Dartmouth, it follows the line of the estuary and offers views up and down the river. The return from the castle is along the coast path, which rises and falls with the cliffs; a flatter alternative is detailed below.

1 Leave the car park the way you drove in. Turn right to take the small lane away from the sea. Follow this lane for about 1km (⅔ mile), crossing a B-Road, to a T-junction with an A-road.

2 There is a footpath on the far side of the road. Turn right. At the end of the footpath, cross the road and take the path opposite, diagonally across a field towards a house. Turn right on the lane in front of the house, then left around its garden and right for a very short section along the road. Turn off along Jawbones Hill and continue along this lane to the water tower.

3 As you approach the water tower, turn right on a tarmac track downhill following signs for Diamond Jubilee Way. When the views open up over Kingswear on the far side of the estuary, turn right through the kissing gate on the Diamond Jubilee Way, heading slightly uphill.

DARTMOUTH CASTLE

> *From here, you can see the two castles flanking the entrance to the River Dart. Behind you, the impressive facade of the Britannia Royal Naval College also comes into view.*

Stay on the path as it descends through deciduous woodland.

> *There are some beautiful springs along this stretch of path.*

At the waymarker, take the flight of steps down to your left, still following the Diamond Jubilee Way. This path leads to the side of the house and bends left to a junction of paths. Turn right to a small lane. Take the steps opposite down to the road below.

BELOW St Petrox church between Points 4 and 5.

4 Turn right along this road and follow it with the river on your left for some distance. Eventually, it bends right towards Warfleet. Follow it around the bend, then turn left onto Castle Road, around the inlet.

> *Surprisingly, the name Warfleet stems from the Saxon name for the stream into the creek and has nothing to do with ships.*

At a road junction, stay left, following signs to Dartmouth Castle. After passing a handful of houses, fork left onto a narrow tarmac drive, following the acorn waymarker. Continue along the path past St Petrox church to the castle.

5 On leaving the castle, head uphill following the acorn waymarker for the coast path, behind the old castle wall and up some steps. At the top of the steps, turn left, then take the middle path below the wall into the woodlands.

(The coast path is very hilly. For an easier return, but with less impressive views, take the lane to the right of the wall, which goes all the way to the car park.)

On the coast path, you will soon pass a brick structure on your right, and there is a steep slope down on your left. Where the path meets the road, stay on the path, pass a couple of benches and then fork right uphill.

At the top of this path, turn left onto the lane and then fork left downhill opposite the house on the right. At the gateposts for Wavenden, fork right. At Compass Cove, bear right uphill, following the acorn waymarker. This is a steep climb, so take your time and enjoy the view. At the waymarker around two-thirds of the way up the slope, there is a

very welcome bench to rest on. Turn left here to continue around the cliffs. At the next junction of paths, either turn left to stay on the route, or right for a slightly shorter route back to the car park. Follow the coast path with the sea on your left

ABOVE View up the River Dart between Points 3 and 4.

BELOW View over Kingswear as seen between Points 3 and 4.

until it eventually turns inland to the car park.

30 DOUNE CASTLE

Some consider Doune Castle to be the best-preserved medieval castle in Scotland. Others may dispute this claim, but it is undoubtedly a fascinating castle to visit. It is strong and imposing but also contains beautiful stonework created by skilled masons who have left their marks on the stone. The courtyard now feels light and spacious. This is in contrast to how it was when the castle was in use. At that time, more stone buildings, wooden structures and stables circled the courtyard. This space was busy and crowded, servicing royal guests as well as legal and estate management functions such as collecting taxes. A trapdoor in the Great Hall was used to drop criminals down into a cell whose only exit was either a rope or a ladder, hence the phrase 'fall from grace'.

Some were lucky and released after just a few days, but the punishment was more severe for others. A gallows tree stood outside the castle gates, used to hang those seen as the worst transgressors. Towards the end of the 19th century, the tree blew down, and the wood was used to make souvenirs, including furniture for the castle.

WALK DETAILS

START/FINISH
Moray Park car park, Doune FK16 6DN

DISTANCE
8.75km (5½ miles)

PARKING
At start and castle

PUBLIC TRANSPORT
Bus from Stirling Railway Station to Bank Street

REFRESHMENTS
Pubs and cafés in Doune

TOILETS
In Moray Park near start

BELOW The view on arrival at the castle.

THE WALK

A relaxing walk alongside Ardoch Burn and the River Teith, which surround three sides of the castle, leads on to a nature reserve where osprey sometimes fish in the loch. Views across the town and to the castle can be seen through the wooded hills as you return.

BELOW The footbridge at the mill between Points 1 and 2.

1 From the car park, turn right onto the lane past the church to Main Street. Turn left. Pass another church on the right, and then take a diagonal right towards Doune Castle. Continue ahead past a row of houses and over a stone bridge. At the end of the road, there is a series of gates. Turn right towards the castle. Cross the footbridge at the mill and continue along the footpath. The castle soon comes into view.

DOUNE CASTLE

> *Look to your right to see the entrance into an old ice house.*

2 The route continues left along the burn until it reaches the River Teith, where it turns upstream. Follow this path for some distance until it reaches the A-road. Turn left (there is a pavement at the side of the road).

> *There's a fabulous view of the castle along the river from the bridge, but please do take care of the traffic if you look.*

3 To continue, do not cross the bridge. Head through the car park on the far side of the road and take the path that follows the line of the river. At the start of the distillery buildings (on the far side of the river), turn diagonally right. This section of path is not clearly defined. Head up the slope until you meet a forest track along the top. Turn left, then turn left again to continue along the top of the valley.

This path arrives at a track into a field. Turn left downhill to a T-junction of tracks. Turn right. Some distance further, turn right at the next T-junction of tracks. The route is now out of forestry land and into farmland. Continue along the track until it eventually reaches the A-road.

4 Turn diagonally right into Doune Woodlands. After about 50m (55yds), at a turning space, turn left along a footpath into the woods. When this footpath returns to a road, continue ahead on the A-road. Cross at the lights and continue in the same direction. At the junction ahead, turn left signposted town centre. Take the first road on the left towards Doune Ponds (Station Wynd), then turn left into the nature reserve. After a few metres, take the left fork past the pond. Join the path around the pond on the right.

> *Keep an eye out for osprey, which have been known to fish in this area.*

At a junction of paths, continue ahead, signposted North Pond. After a few metres, bear left, sticking to the wider path. Follow the path around North Pond, keeping the water on your right. When you reach a surfaced path, turn left and left again after about 15m (50ft). Turn left onto the next section of surfaced path and up a flight of steps. At the top, make your way over to the grassy knoll.

> *You will see the church and, to the right of that, the castle is just visible above the trees.*

5 Turn downhill on the stony track. After a short distance, turn left up a footpath signposted Commonty Walk, with a meadow on the right. As you rise, the castle eventually comes

ABOVE The castle from Commonty Walk between Points 5 and 6.

BELOW Fly fishing on the River Teith.

back into view, this time on the left of the church.

The hills behind are the Gargunnock Hills, with the Campsie Fells to the right.

At the road, turn right. Pass a track on the left, and then after another 50m (55yds), turn left down through the woods, past a bench, to the tarmac cycle path below. Turn right and follow the cycle path until the bridge over the minor road. Turn left after the bridge to return to the car park.

31 DOVER CASTLE

Although most of the town was destroyed by German bombers in WWII, Dover Castle was not touched. Perhaps they didn't realise what an important place it was – or more likely, perhaps one of the German generals wanted to claim it for himself after the war.

What we see today is mainly the work of the Normans a century or so after their successful conquest of England. However, there is also a Saxon church and the remains of a Roman lighthouse on the site, as well as more modern additions.

The Great Tower is colourfully decorated as it would have been towards the end of the 12th century, putting paid to the idea that castles were grim and grey.

One of the remarkable things about Dover Castle is its extensive tunnelling. First, tunnels were built in the medieval period. These were added to during the Napoleonic Wars in the late 18th and early 19th centuries. During WWII, the Napoleonic Wars tunnels were once again used, this time as a field hospital and an important command centre. The more modern tunnels are

WALK DETAILS

START/FINISH
Dover Priory railway station, CT17 9SB

DISTANCE
8.75km (5½ miles)

PARKING
At start, National Trust White Cliffs of Dover car park CT16 1HJ (join at Point 6) and between Points 7 & 8

PUBLIC TRANSPORT
Train to Dover Priory railway station

REFRESHMENTS
Pubs and cafés in Dover, café at start, café at Point 6

TOILETS
At Point 6

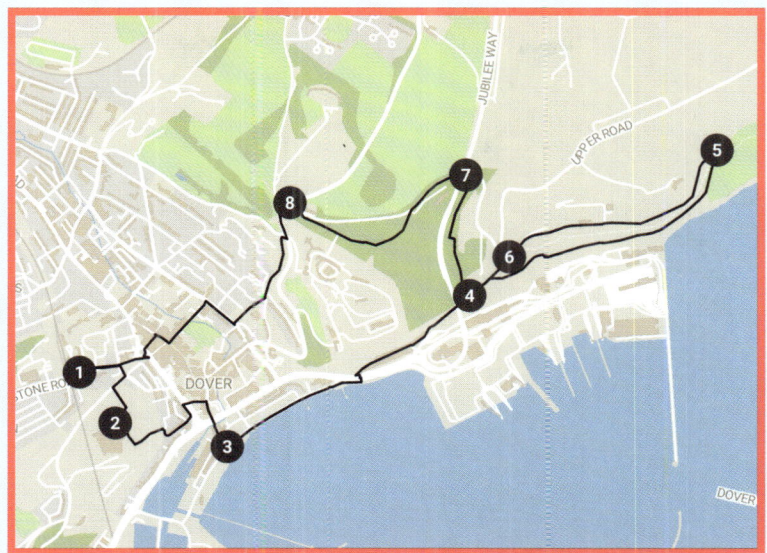

open for timed tours, and visitors to the castle can explore the older ones freely.

THE WALK

A challenging walk with steep ascents and descents. The effort is well rewarded, with spectacular views of the castle and the White Cliffs. The walk can be split into two loops, one around the castle, town and fort, and the other along the cliffs. Both have fantastic views of the castle.

1 From the ticket office, turn right past the Priory Hotel. Turn left at the main road then right up steps, just past Christchurch Court. Turn right onto North Military Road. Opposite Castle View bungalow, turn left up steep steps. At the first junction of paths, continue up the steps. At the second, turn right uphill to the fort.

2 Turn left towards the sea. Where the path forks, turn left downhill. At the gate on the right, descend the steps opposite. The castle is ahead. At the end of the path, turn right. Follow this road to the left and straight downhill to a dual carriageway. Cross at the traffic lights to your left, then continue ahead downhill. At King Street, turn right and use the underpass to reach the seafront.

BELOW Dover Castle enjoys a prominent position.

3 Turn left and walk with the sea on your right until you reach a major road. Cross at the traffic lights ahead. The windows of the castle tunnels are in the cliffs above you. Turn right behind the houses, on East Cliff. At the end of the row, continue ahead past garages. The cliffs are rising on your left. Follow this path as it ascends, passing underneath the flyover. Just before a flight of steps, there is a path on the left. (If you started in Dover and wish to shorten the walk, turn left here.)

4 The route follows the path uphill for a little longer and turns right at the gate by the Langdon Cliffs sign. (Continue uphill for a direct route to the White Cliffs of Dover car park.) Follow the chalk path along the cliffs. At a viewing point, turn right then left onto a path that gradually descends. At the bottom, continue with the sea on your right. Pass the Langdon Hole sign and continue to a junction of paths.

5 Turn sharp left on a well-made path with steps up, that passes in front of the coastguard station. The sea is on your left. Follow the path through the car park to a road.

6 Keep left to take a steep path downhill. At the junction of paths a few metres after a flight of steps, you have reached Point 4 again. Turn right, away from the docks. After about 700m (½ mile), at a junction of paths, turn left to reach a road.

7 Turn left to follow this road for around 300m (330yds). At the first junction, turn diagonal left on a path heading downhill, signposted Blériot Memorial.

Continue past the memorial. At a T-junction of paths, turn right to and through a car park to a road. At the road, continue uphill to a T-junction. The castle is behind you.

8 Turn left onto this road. To visit the castle, take the first road on the left. To continue on the route, descend the steps on the far side of Connaught Road. Head downhill with the wall on your right.

At the end of the path, continue ahead for 20m (65ft), then take a footpath between walls, heading diagonally right downhill.

At the end of the path, turn right along the road, then take the first road on the left. Follow this road past a park, around to the right and then around to the left onto Priory Street. Head straight over the roundabout to return to the station.

(If you started at the White Cliffs of Dover car park, turn left up the steps opposite the petrol station and follow from Point 1.)

LEFT Windows in the castle tunnels as seen between Points 3 and 4.

INSET Western Heights Fort (seen at Point 2).

RIGHT The Blériot Memorial between Points 7 and 8.

DOVER CASTLE

32 DUMBARTON CASTLE

Dumbarton Castle was once close to the border with Norway, but it was a stronghold well before that.

After the Romans left in the 5th century, Dumbarton became the centre of the kingdom of Strathclyde. In 1034, when Duncan of Strathclyde became King of Scotland, the kingdom integrated with Scotland, and the fortification at Dumbarton became defunct.

In 1098, when Argyll and the Hebrides were lost to Norway, Dumbarton became strategically important again. By 1222, a new castle had been built, presumably to support the return of Argyll and the Hebrides to Scottish rule. This was finally achieved in 1266.

In the centuries following, the castle was used to shelter future monarchs (King David II and Mary, Queen of Scots) while they awaited rescue by the French, under threat from their English adversaries. In 1523, a French invasion force was garrisoned at the castle but left a few months later without actioning their plans.

Standing on near-vertical basaltic cliffs, the castle appears unassailable, but as with Edinburgh Castle

WALK DETAILS

START/FINISH
Dumbarton Central railway station, G82 1PZ

DISTANCE
8km (5 miles)

PARKING
Car parks in Dumbarton

PUBLIC TRANSPORT
Train to Dumbarton Central or Dumbarton East (join walk at Point 2)

REFRESHMENTS
Pubs and cafés in Dumbarton, café at Maritime Museum between Points 3 & 4, café in Levengrove Park near Point 5

TOILETS
In castle (after entry gate)

RIGHT The 18th century Governor's House in the castle.

BELOW Dumbarton Castle stands on near-vertical basaltic cliffs.

(see Walk 36), this once proved to be its downfall. In 1571, 100 men scaled up the north-east side and took the guards by surprise, winning the castle by stealth rather than muscle.

THE WALK
Follow the foreshore of the Firth of Clyde with great views of the castle as you approach it. Afterwards, you get a second fantastic view of the castle, this time from the park where

DUMBARTON CASTLE

the remains of Robert the Bruce are buried. This walk is almost entirely on flat tarmac.

1 **From the train platform, head down the ramp and turn right to exit past platform 1.** Turn right along the road. Continue ahead over the crossroads. At the T-junction, turn left and then right onto Crosslet Road.

Immediately after the school, turn right down a tarmac footpath. On the far side of the clubhouse, turn right to a road.

2 **Head across the grass straight in front of you, and then turn right under the railway bridge.**

At the next road, kink left and then right. Just before the gates into an industrial yard, turn right onto a footpath signposted Dumbarton Foreshore.

Follow the stream to a footbridge on the right and cross it.

Turn left along the foreshore to the castle rock.

3 **At the road, turn left for the castle or right to continue along the route.** Turn left at the mini roundabout, then follow the road around to the right to a T-junction. Turn left. Head straight over the next roundabout and turn left along the front of the Scottish Maritime Museum. At the end of the building, turn left towards the castle and then right along the shore.

This is another fantastic viewing point. There is also some public art here, celebrating the glorious history of Dumbarton by way of firsts. These include the building of the first commercial ship powered by steam turbines, the first prototype hovercraft, the first helicopter and the building of the Cutty Sark. A pair of tusks, referencing the town symbol of an elephant, neatly frame the castle from here too.

The path turns to the right alongside the River Leven. Follow the path

along the river to the bridge.

4 Cross here, looking left for another view of the castle. On the far side of the bridge, cross the first road then take the next road to the left to the gates of the park. Enter the park here, then turn right after the Gatekeeper's Lodge and follow this path around the outside edge of the park, past an exotic selection of trees, until you reach the foreshore.

5 Continue towards the castle. Some distance further, with the castle on your right, follow the path between a sports pitch and a boat yard. The path ends at a tarmac drive. Turn left. Past Rowanlea, take the gated entrance back into the park. Once inside, turn left and then right up to the ruins of St Serf's Church.

It is believed that this is where the embalmed viscera (organs) of King Robert I (Robert the Bruce) are buried, except for his heart. His dying wish was that his heart be taken to Jerusalem, to fulfil a solemn oath he took to take part in the Crusades.

6 Continue to the bandstand, and head right. At the next junction of paths, head towards the bridge and re-cross the river.

The view to the left is up to Loch Lomond and the Trossachs National Park, which has 21 Munros (mountains over 3,000ft/915m), and a similar number of Corbetts (mountains from 2,500–3,000ft/760-915m). The national park is huge – 1,865 square km (720 square miles), but the River Leven is only 9.5km (6 miles) long, from Loch Lomond to the Forth of Clyde.

Head straight across the junction at the end of the bridge, onto Risk Street. Turn left at the pedestrian crossing signposted Dumbarton Central station. The station and end of the walk are visible in the distance ahead.

FAR LEFT The path to the castle from Dumbarton Foreshore between Points 2 and 3.

LEFT The ruins of St Serf's church between Points 5 and 6.

BELOW A pair of tusks on the foreshore neatly frames the castle, as seen between Points 3 and 4.

33 DUNNOTTAR CASTLE

Dunnottar Castle stands in a stunning and precarious location, perched on pudding stone – a conglomerate of boulders and stones held within a cementing material – that forms a headland jutting into the North Sea.

In the 5th century, a small church was established on the site by St Ninian, and Picts inhabited the area until the 9th century. A stone tower was built here in the late 14th century, but the castle did not really come into its own until after the British Civil Wars. In 1649, Oliver Cromwell destroyed the English crown jewels and set his sights on Scotland (and Ireland).

The Scottish crown jewels, known as the Honours of Scotland, were sent to Dunnottar for safekeeping. By 1652, the whole of Scotland had fallen to Cromwell's men – apart from Dunnottar, which was under siege. The castle held for eight months. The invaders were intent on destroying the crown jewels, but when they entered the castle, the Honours were nowhere to be found. Luckily, someone had had the foresight to smuggle them out of the castle, which means that they survived and are now the oldest crown jewels in Britain. The Honours of Scotland are on display in Edinburgh Castle (see Walk 36).

WALK DETAILS

START/FINISH
Stonehaven Market Square, AB39 2BY

DISTANCE
7.5km (4⅔ miles)

PARKING
At start, at castle

PUBLIC TRANSPORT
Train to Stonehaven

REFRESHMENTS
Pubs and cafés in Stonehaven

TOILETS
At the harbour

BELOW Dunnottar Castle is perched on a headland jutting into the North Sea (credit: iStock).

The Walk

The route to the castle takes you along the beach, past the old harbour and up onto cliffs. This gives some tremendous views of the castle and its setting atop a small peninsula. The return leg heads inland, along a quiet lane through farmland, then down through Dunnottar Woods back into the town.

1 From the marketplace, head down Market Lane to the shore. Turn right along the beach and then around the bay to the car park by the harbour. Turn right around the harbour.

Stonehaven Harbour was first built at the turn of the 17th century, and has been destroyed by the sea and rebuilt several times since then. The final rebuilding was at the start of the 19th century. Over its lifetime, the harbour has been used to import coal and limestone and export grain, potatoes, fish and whisky. These days, Stonehaven Harbour is home to a few small fishing boats, but is now mainly recreational and there is no longer a fish market in the town.

At Hogmanay (Scottish New Year), the harbour is lit up by the Stonehaven Fireballs Festival, where local people parade through the streets, swinging a lit fireball around their heads. This spectacular event has been entertaining –

DUNNOTTAR CASTLE

ABOVE Dunnottar War Memorial (credit: iStock).

and possibly singeing – crowds for over a hundred years. It is said to burn away any bad luck from the old year and allow space for good luck in the new year.

2 Pass the Ship Inn and continue to Wallace Wynd. Turn right here, signposted Dunnottar Castle. At the end of the passage, turn left. Continue uphill until you reach the road. Turn left, with the shore below on your left. Where the road bends sharply to the right, continue ahead on the tarmac path between fields.

As you reach the gate to the war memorial, the castle comes into view along the coast. This war memorial is somewhat more impressive than the average. Eight Doric columns with supporting lintels surround the stones of remembrance. The stones themselves are raised on blocks and list 163 soldiers who died in WWI, 36 who died in WWII and 12 civilians who also died in WWII. The memorial is perched high on the cliffs, in a prominent position over the town.

3 The tarmac path now becomes a stone path, which is easy to follow around the coast all the way to the castle.

4 At the castle's fence, turn left to visit the castle or right to continue on the route. From the castle car park, turn right onto the road and then left up a farm track with the farm buildings on your left. When you reach the A-road, carefully cross to the far side and turn left. There is space to walk off the road. After about 350m (380yds), turn right down another quiet lane. Cross the bridge, then turn right into Dunnottar Woods car park.

5 Head past the information board into the woods. Stick to the wide woodland track, leading along the side of the valley, with red waymarkers. When you reach the drive to Dunnottar Park, follow the track around to the right and down to a tarmac lane. Cross the lane and continue ahead, again following the red waymarker posts. Turn right

through the car park, still following the red trail. Turn left when you reach the grassy area ahead, then head up a small slope into the trees. Through the trees, take the path straight along the middle of the meadow ahead, under some powerlines and back into woods. Turn right to head downhill. This path leads to a tarmac lane. Turn left then right to cross a stream on a footbridge. Take the footpath ahead between houses, along a row of garages, across another road and then up a slope. At the top of the steps, turn right. Follow this road back to the start.

ABOVE Stonehaven harbour (credit: iStock).

BELOW The stone path along the coast to the castle.

34 DUNSTAFFNAGE & DUNOLLIE CASTLES

Many castles were built on old fortifications, and Dunstaffnage is no exception. It was erected by Duncan MacDougall around 1220 on land that lay between Scotland and Norway. The MacDougalls were of mixed Norse and Gaelic origin, with no fixed allegiance to either country.

Stone blocks were grafted onto a rocky outcrop to create walls almost 3.5m (11½ft) thick to an impressive height. The castle was also surrounded by a broad and deep ditch; it provided a formidable challenge to enemy attackers. The fortification would not have been hidden in the trees as it is now, and like many others of its time, it was also whitewashed to make it more striking.

The chapel in the woods is considered one of the best contemporary examples, indicating the wealth and status of the MacDougalls. Their power in the region did not last, though; the castle changed hands several times before finally ending up in the guardianship of Historic Scotland.

WALK DETAILS

START/FINISH
Ocean Explorer Centre car park, Dunbeg PA37 1QA

DISTANCE
10.75km (6⅔ miles)

PARKING
At start

PUBLIC TRANSPORT
Bus from Oban Railway Station to MacCallum Court (join at Lochnell Road between Points 1 & 2)

REFRESHMENTS
On campus at start, at Ganavan Sands car park and at Dunollie Castle (after entry gate)

TOILETS
Both castles (after entry gate), Ganavan Sands car park

BELOW Dunollie Castle (credit: iStock).

Nearby Dunollie Castle was built around 200 years later, also by the MacDougalls. Although younger and more ruinous than Dunstaffnage, this is the castle that acted as the nerve centre of the MacDougalls' realm.

However, this site was of great importance long before the MacDougalls arrived. A Neolithic flint scraper indicates it was used as early as 4000–2000 BC. During the 6th to 8th centuries AD, Dunollie was one of the seats of power of the kingdom of Dalriada, which stretched along the western shores of Scotland and over to what is now County Antrim in Northern Ireland. We know that the local king, Selbach, rebuilt Dunollie in AD 714, having razed the previous fortification during a power struggle with his brother. An ancient footstone was found at the base of the MacDougall castle, which is thought to have been used in coronation ceremonies during the Dalriada period.

BELOW Dunstaffnage Castle.

DUNSTAFFNAGE & DUNOLLIE CASTLES

The Walk

Stroll from Scotland's Marine Science campus on an undulating hard cycle track through quiet meadows and woodland to Ganavan Sands. The next stop is Dunollie Castle, garden and museum perched on a basalt mound with terrific views of Mull and Oban. Then, return via a clifftop hike to Dunstaffnage Castle.

1 Walk back through the university campus towards the A-road. About 20m (65ft) after the speed limit sign, turn right up a gravel drive. At the end, take the narrow grassy footpath uphill between houses. At the parking area, turn right and follow Castle Road to a T-junction. Turn right onto Lochnell Road. Take the first road on the right through another parking area to and through a gate at the far end.

> *You are now in open countryside, on a shared pedestrian and cycle path. You will soon see Lismore Lighthouse ahead, with the low-lying island of the same name to its right and the Isle of Mull behind.*

Continue to the bay and beachside car park.

2 Head up the road between houses. This is a quiet road that shortly returns to the shore and follows it. There are two short stretches that do not have a pavement, but the traffic is generally light and slow.

> *You can see the marina on Kerrera over the water and the outskirts of Oban ahead.*

Where the pavement runs out for a second time, Dunollie Castle is on the hill to your left. Continue around the headland, then turn left along the castle drive to visit it.

3 Retrace your steps to Ganavan Bay, Point 2.

For the return leg of the walk, head along the bay past the end of the car park onto a path along the shore. Take a few steps up at the end of the beach and continue along the path ahead until the first set of cliffs ends and you reach a small stream.

4 Just before the path crosses the stream, turn right inland. At the top of the rise, turn left through bracken uphill and then bear left to reach the clifftop.

There is an incredible view from the top. The first sizeable island on the left is Kerrera, then the Isle of Mull is a little further around to the right. The lighthouse is on Lismore, with the mainland behind it. Ahead and to the right, the highest of the mountains you can see is Ben Cruachan (see Kilchurn Castle, Walk 48).

Where the path splits by Ganavan Hill, you can either go around it towards the sea or over the top. Both paths rejoin a little later. Continue ahead up the next hill.

From here, you can just make out Dunstaffnage Castle in the trees on the peninsula ahead.

The Falls of Lora are visible slightly to the right, underneath the grey angular Connel Bridge.

Turn left off the hill towards the water. The path leads down to the right and arrives at a gravel cycle path. Turn left and follow the cycle path around the shore until you reach the bay with the university buildings to your right. From the beach, either turn right along the edge of the woodland back to the car park or, to visit the castle, continue ahead into the woods, following a sometimes faint path around the shore.

ABOVE The shared pedestrian and cycle path between Points 1 and 2.

BELOW View across the Firth of Lorn.

35 DURHAM CASTLE

It is thought that Durham's first fortification on this site was associated with the body of St Cuthbert (see Walk 4, Bamburgh Castle). Viking raids along the coast made the monks uneasy about its safety on Lindisfarne, so they moved it around Northumbria, looking for a suitable resting place. St Cuthbert came to one of them in a vision and advised that he wished to be taken to the uninhabited peninsula created by a loop in the River Wear at Durham. The monks duly obliged, and it is thought that Uhtred the Bold brought men from Bamburgh to clear the site and create a fortification across the northern end of the peninsula to protect the new monastery.

Nothing remains of these early buildings. About 75 years later, by the command of William the Conqueror, the Normans built a castle here to keep the powerful local noblemen in check, and help defend England against Scottish incursions.

William then installed Prince Bishops at Durham. These wealthy men held immense power, being the only people apart from the king who could set taxes, mint coins and hold legal courts. The castle served as both a fortification and a palace, and has seen many changes over the centuries.

WALK DETAILS

START/FINISH
Durham Castle, DH1 3RW

DISTANCE
7.5km (4⅔ miles)

PARKING
Durham City Park and Ride

PUBLIC TRANSPORT
Train or coach to Durham

REFRESHMENTS
Pubs and cafés in Durham, café in cathedral

TOILETS
Palace Green at start

BELOW Durham Castle keep (credit: iStock).

THE WALK

A countryside walk from the centre of an important city. Enjoy watching the wildlife and watersports along the River Wear and wandering through the city's abundant woodlands to return to the river again, with incredible views of the cathedral and castle. An easy walk, mainly on pavement and woodland paths.

1 From the entrance to Durham Castle, turn left then left again down Owengate. At the T-junction, turn left onto Saddler Street. Take the first road on the right, down some steps. Immediately before Elvet Bridge, head down the steps on your left and

BELOW Durham Castle gatehouse.

DURHAM CASTLE

walk along the riverside, with the river on your right.

As you walk along the river, you will notice several rowing clubs and may see people out on the river. There are 16 college rowing clubs in the university, and these make up around half of all the rowers in the North East.

Continue along the river for 2km (1¼ miles), to a footbridge.

2 Cross the river. Turn right through a gate, then immediately left just inside the woods, with the hill rising to your right. As you near the road, take the waymarked path that rises up the hill. Follow it around to the right, to the top of the hill.

BELOW Rowing on the River Weir is a popular pastime as well as sport.

BELOW RIGHT Durham Cathedral (credit: iStock).

You are now on Maiden Castle, the site of an Iron Age fort that used the steep slopes on three sides of the hill as protection against attack.

Follow the path around the summit, down the side of a field, through a hedge and across the next field. When you reach the line of trees at the top of this hill, turn left. Immediately after the last tree, turn left. When you reach the woods, continue downhill back to the path at the bottom. Turn right and follow the path to the road.

3 Cross the road and continue ahead into the woods on a flat path. After some distance, there is a junction next to a bench. Stay right, heading uphill. This path eventually rises to meet Hollingside Lane, where there are a few parking spaces. Turn right, past the botanic gardens. Where the lane bends to the left, take the tarmac path on the right. Follow it around to

the left. At the car park, continue straight ahead down a narrow path into woodland. After about 3m, turn left onto a faint path that shortly bends to the right and follows the edge of the woodland. Where the path bends to the right again, exit through the hedge and turn right onto the tarmac path, then right again down through the edge of the woods. When you reach the buildings, turn left to the road.

4 Turn right along the road, cross then continue downhill. At the junction with traffic lights, turn left, then right down the public footpath on the far side of the bus shelter, past a cricket pitch and down to the river. Reaching the river, continue ahead with the river on your right.

> After the first bridge, there are fantastic views of the cathedral on the far side of the river. On the approach to the second bridge, the castle also comes into view to your right.

Cross the river at the second bridge. Turn down some steps on the far side of the first building on the right, then fork left signposted Cathedral and Castle. At the top of this path, turn left between buildings to return to the start. The castle is on your left, and the cathedral on your right.

> The cathedral is home to the relics of St Cuthbert and remains a site of pilgrimage. Four of the Northern Saints Trails long-distance pilgrimage routes finish here. The importance of the castle and cathedral were recognised when they were inscribed on the World Heritage List in 1986. UNESCO describes the cathedral as 'the largest and most perfect monument of "Norman" style architecture in England'.

36 EDINBURGH CASTLE

Castle Rock has been inhabited for at least 3,000 years, since the Bronze Age. It became a hill fort in the Iron Age, and local chieftains lived here during the Roman occupation.

Edinburgh Castle stands on vertical rock faces almost all the way around, which makes it appear impenetrable. It is, in fact, Britain's most besieged castle, and of its 26 sieges, most were successful. One small party of men even entered from the rocks on the north side, surprised the defenders and quickly overwhelmed them.

Highlights of the castle include St Margaret's Chapel, one of the oldest buildings in Edinburgh and also the castle's oldest. The chapel dates from the same period as Duddingston Kirk at the far point of the walk. Mons Meg, Britain's largest gun, is no longer in use, although another gun is still fired most days. This is the One O'Clock Gun, used since 1861 to enable ships in the Firth of Forth to set their clocks.

The Stone of Destiny, which has been used for kingmaking ceremonies since the time of the early Picts, now resides at Edinburgh Castle alongside the Honours of Scotland. These are the oldest crown jewels in the British Isles, as the English ones were sold or

WALK DETAILS

START/FINISH
Edinburgh Castle, EH1 2NG

DISTANCE
9km (5⅔ miles)

PARKING
City centre, Holyrood car park EH8 8AZ at Point 2, a few spaces near Duddingston at Point 5

PUBLIC TRANSPORT
Train to Edinburgh Waverley or coach to Edinburgh

REFRESHMENTS
Pubs and cafés in Edinburgh, pub at Duddingston

TOILETS
At castle (before entry gate)

BELOW Edinburgh Castle from the south.

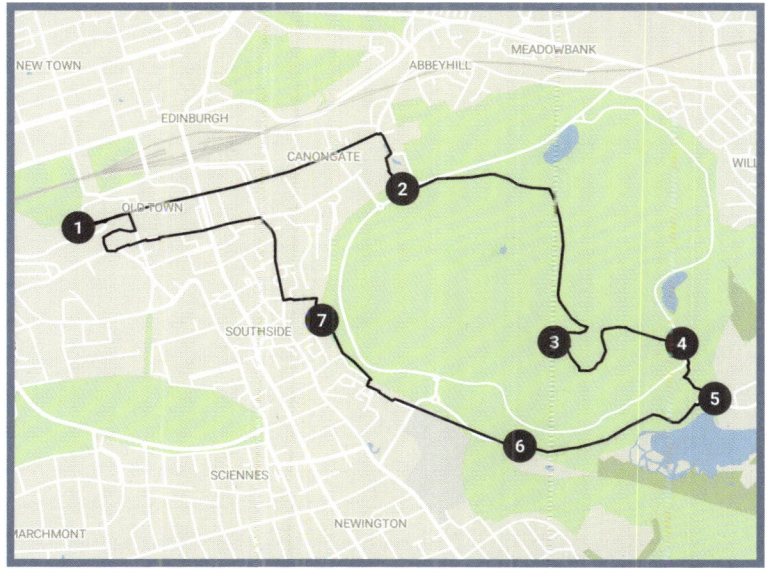

melted down into coins when the monarchy was dissolved at the end of the British Civil Wars.

THE WALK

This walk follows Edinburgh's Royal Mile, ascends a sometimes steep and rocky path to Arthur's Seat, then visits Duddingston, home to a 900-year-old church and the Sheep Heid pub, reputedly frequented by Mary, Queen of Scots. It returns to the city via a wildlife-rich loch and disused railway tunnel.

1 From the castle, walk down the full length of the road ahead – the Royal Mile. At the mini roundabout, turn right between the Palace of Holyroodhouse and the Scottish Parliament.

Arthur's Seat is visible ahead.

Cross the road around the hill then turn left on the pavement.

BELOW Arthur's Seat (credit: iStock).

EDINBURGH CASTLE 157

2 **25m (80ft) after the zebra crossing, take the gently rising tarmac path that forks right into the park.** After about 275m (300yds), take the left fork onto a dirt path.

> As the path rises, you will see St Margaret's Loch to the left with the ruins of St Anthony's Chapel above it.

Follow this wide stony path, sometimes with steps, as it rises to a flat viewpoint near the summit of Arthur's Seat. Follow the path to the right and continue uphill until you reach the trig point and location finder at the summit.

3 **To continue, head towards the castle, which sits on a volcanic plug to the west.** After a few metres, turn back on yourself to the left. Take one of the paths to the grassy dip between two smaller peaks. Ascend the craggy left-hand peak, Crow Hill. Continue in the same direction, then drop left back down towards the viewpoint. When you reach the wide grassy path, turn right downhill between Crow Hill above and Dunsapie Loch below.

> At the road, look back to see the ancient cultivation terraces.

4 **Turn right along the road. At a bench just before the railings, take the steps down to the left.** Follow this path to the right and down to the road. You are now at the edge of Duddingston, close to the church. The pub is a little further into the village.

5 **Cross the road and take the steps ahead to a seating area overlooking the loch, an important wildlife reserve.** Exit the seating area down more steps. At the bottom, turn right onto a path that rises through a gate to the road. Turn left and follow the pavement alongside the road for around 1km (⅔ mile).

6 **About 25m (80ft) beyond the end of the railings, take the steps down to the left, then turn left again into the Innocent Railway Tunnel.**

This was the first railway tunnel in Scotland, now converted into a walk- and cycleway.

After around 500m (⅓ mile), the path emerges into a residential area, the site of the first railway station in Edinburgh. At the far end of the car park, turn right onto the road to continue walking in the same direction. When the road bears left, continue straight. After 65m (70yds), turn right up steps and enter the woodland ahead. Turn left onto a path along the top of the slope. After passing a long stone building on the left, turn left through some railings and drop down to a bike park

7 Skirt around the bike park to exit on the far side. Turn right downhill on the tarmac path. Take the first road on the left (Brown Street, but there are no signs) and follow it to a T-junction. Turn right onto Pleasance.

As the road heads downhill, the tower on the ridge in front of you is the Nelson Monument on Calton Hill.

At the crossroads with traffic lights, turn left onto Cowgate. Continue along this road to a mini roundabout.

Look up for a view of the castle high ahead.

Turn right, then follow the road around to the right.

At the end of this road, turn left, then left again onto the Royal Mile to complete the walk.

LEFT Duddingston Kirk, near Point 5.
BELOW West Bow, between Point 7 and the castle.

EDINBURGH CASTLE

37 EILEAN DONAN CASTLE

Eilean Donan is instantly recognisable, as it has featured in many films, including *Highlander* (1986) and *The World is Not Enough* (1999). Eilean Donan is a tidal island connected to the mainland by its iconic bridge.

The original castle is thought to have been built in the first half of the 13th century. The hornwork – the structure that juts towards the bridge – was added during the 16th century to protect the well and create a mounting for defensive cannons.

Unfortunately, not much of the original castle survived the Jacobite Rising of 1719. In 1718, Spain and Britain embarked on one of several wars between the two countries. The Spaniards supported the Jacobites in Scotland to create a pincer movement that would make a successful invasion more likely. The army attacking England foundered in a storm, and just a few hundred troops landed in Scotland. They were headquartered in Eilean Donan Castle and used it to store provisions and ammunition. While the troops were distracted in battle, the Royal Navy took the opportunity to bombard the castle, ultimately causing its destruction.

WALK DETAILS

START/FINISH
Dornie Community Hall car park, IV40 8DY

DISTANCE
8km (5 miles)

PARKING
At start and at castle

PUBLIC TRANSPORT
Bus from Inverness bus station or Portree to Bridge Road End (Dornie)

REFRESHMENTS
Café at castle, pub and hotel in Dornie, café at start (not open every day)

TOILETS
At start and at castle (before entry gate)

RIGHT Eilean Donan Castle.

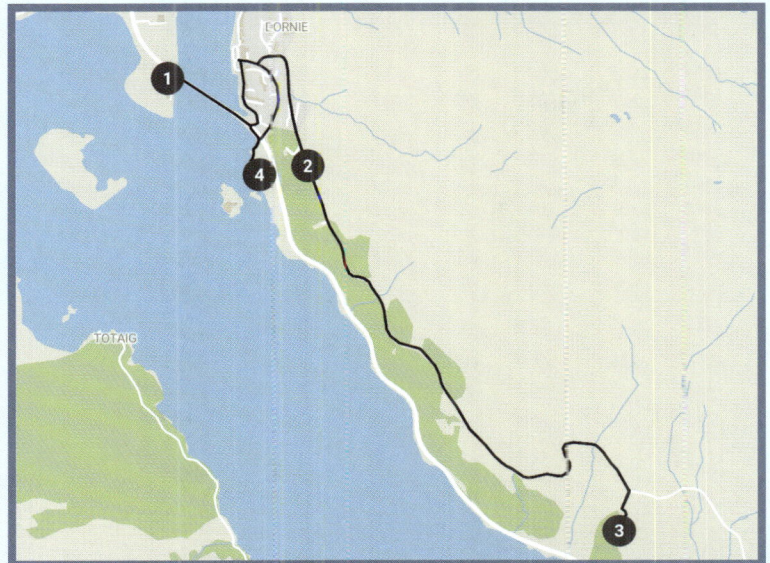

It was not until the 20th century that the castle was rebuilt as a close replica of the original.

THE WALK

Walk into Dornie, past a pub and hotel, leading onto a gradual, quiet road climb to the famous castle viewing point. Look up for views of Skye, Kyle of Lochalsh and Inner Sound. More views and peace on the return trip. Optional attractive stroll along Loch Long with traditional Scottish homes.

1 From the car park, turn right over the bridge towards the village of Dornie. On the far side of the bridge, take the footpath left to pass a community garden to the shore. Continue in front of the brightly coloured houses past the pub.

Dornie stands at the confluence of three lochs: Duich to the south-east, Long to the north-east and Alsh to the west, meeting the sea. This made it the ideal location for a fishing village, although it no longer has a fishing fleet. Road traffic to Skye used to travel through the village, crossing Loch Long by ferry until a bridge was built. It is now significantly quieter as most traffic passes it by.

Turn right at the Dornie Hotel. (To extend your walk, continue past the hotel along the side of Loch Long and return when you are ready.) Pass the hotel car park and turn left on the minor road signposted Carr Brae Viewpoint. (We will return to this point.)

Follow this quiet road uphill until you reach the viewpoint of the castle and Kyle of Lochalsh to the right.

The land immediately behind the castle is mainland Scotland, but the mountain further behind and to the right is on the Isle of Skye.

2 Continue up the lane for about 2km (1¼ miles), past the quirky house with a boat extension. A short distance later, look for the lay-by and gate in the fence on the right for the next viewpoint.

From here, you have far-reaching views along Loch Duich in both directions. The three lochs – Duich, Long and Alsh – make up a Marine Protected Area (MPA). One of the reasons for their importance is that they support flame shell beds. Flame shells are bivalve molluscs (with two connected shells) that hide on the seafloor in nests made from other shells and stones. When they crowd together, they form a raised platform that protects the seabed and provides a habitat for many other species, including algae and invertebrates. This habitat mainly occurs on the west coast of Scotland, and Loch Alsh has some of the best extensive flame shell beds. They can be damaged by mechanical means such as trawling, which is why the loch is protected.

The other reason for the lochs' protected status is the burrowed mud that they support. This might seem somewhat less attractive to us, but provides an important habitat for creatures such as the Norway lobster and burrowing brittlestars (related to starfish, with longer legs). This fragile habitat can be damaged by physical disturbance and water pollution.

Fish farming is still permitted in the loch, despite the damage it can do to sensitive habitats as described above. Tens of thousands of fish live in the nets, which can pose challenges in terms of food, disease, animal welfare and pollution from the fish's faeces, their food and chemical waste.

Glen Shiel extends from the end of Loch Duich to the left for about 14.5km (9 miles) to Loch Cluanie. Towards the far

end is the site of the Battle of Glen Shiel, the only battle of the 1719 Jacobite uprising against the British crown. Although the battle took place some 25km (16 miles) from Eilean Donan Castle, the castle's role in the uprising, which was effectively quashed by the British armed forces, led to its destruction.

3 Retrace your steps back down to the village. At the T-junction, turn left to visit the castle.

4 From the castle, turn towards then across the bridge to complete the walk.

TOP Loch Duich.
ABOVE The quiet lane above the loch.
BELOW The outlook from the viewpoint at Point 2.

38 FARLEIGH HUNGERFORD CASTLE

Farleigh Hungerford Castle was built by Sir Thomas Hungerford in the late 14th century as a fortified mansion on the site of an old manor, more to impress than as a fortress. At that time, you needed permission from the king to fortify your home, which had not been sought. However, Sir Thomas received nothing more than a royal pardon for this misdemeanour.

This was possibly the smallest of the scandals to beset the castle's owners. Other tales include murder, Rapunzel-style imprisonment and beheadings.

The castle is mostly in ruins because when it was sold towards the end of the 17th century, the new owners reused the stone to build a modern house nearby rather than trying to make the draughty old building habitable.

The chapel is the most intact building left on site and well worth a visit. It was built by Sir Thomas Hungerford as the village church, then replaced with another in the village when the castle was extended. The family vault beneath the chapel contains unique lead coffins with faces moulded into them. Within the chapel is a 15th-century wall painting of St George, probably commissioned when the 1st Lord Hungerford became a Knight of the Garter.

WALK DETAILS

START/FINISH
Belcombe Road Parking, Avoncliff BA15 2HD

DISTANCE
8.5km (5¼ miles)

PARKING
At start, a few spaces at Avoncliff railway station, at castle

PUBLIC TRANSPORT
Trains to Avoncliff (start) or Freshford (join walk at Point 6)

REFRESHMENTS
Café and pub at start

TOILETS
No public toilets on route

BELOW The castle's south-east tower (credit: M Reel/Shutterstock).

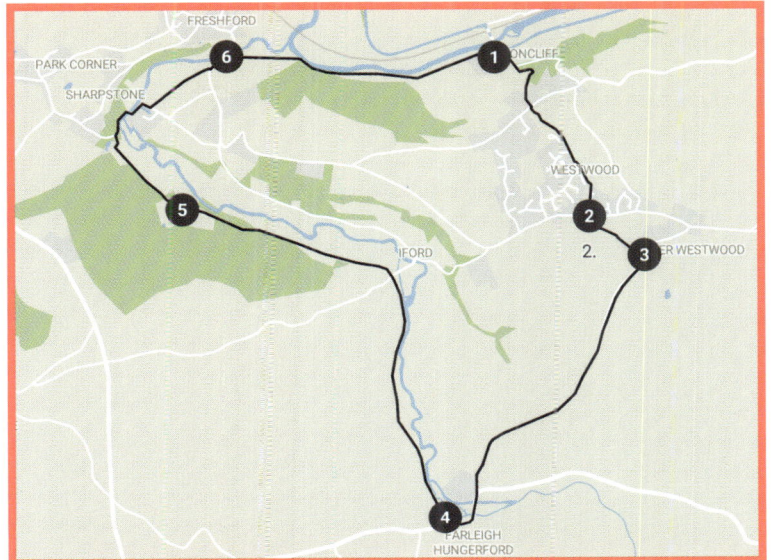

THE WALK

An easy and delightful walk through picturesque English countryside. This route crosses lively streams and more staid rivers, and traverses meadows and woodlands full of wildflowers and wildlife. All this, in rolling hills speckled with golden stone houses. Parts of the path can get muddy.

1 From the car park, turn right uphill, following the lane ahead and then to the right. Where the lane bends left, continue straight ahead onto the footpath. At the fork, head either way – both options meet a little further up. When you reach a tarmac lane, continue uphill for a short distance to a T-junction. Cross the road, and follow the winding path ahead through the park. Keep the children's playground on your right and exit the park on a path that runs to the left of some gardens.

At the end of this path, continue ahead on a residential street. After 40m (44yds), take the small gate through the hedge and turn right with the hedge on your right. When

ABOVE The 15th century mural of St George in the castle's chapel.

the path bends to the left, bear right through another gate onto a footpath. Turn left onto the path.

FARLEIGH HUNGERFORD CASTLE 165

Continue in the same direction until you reach a road.

2 Dogleg right then left, through a gate, then downhill with the fence on your right. Turn left when you meet another fence, walking between a house and a paddock. Follow the path through another gate and between hedges. At the nursery, follow the signs between the greenhouses, bearing right off their drive. After the greenhouses, cross a track and keep the fence on your right until the path rejoins the drive. Turn right. After about 20m (65ft), turn left through a gap in the hedge to join another footpath. Turn right onto this path, to reach a junction at Manor Cottage.

3 Step over the metal stile to the left of the cottage and follow the footpath around to the right, behind it. Keep the hedgerow on your right. Eventually, the path enters a woodland and then reaches a road. Turn left and follow the road for 1km (⅔ mile) until you reach Farleigh Hungerford. Turn right to cross the river over two separate bridges. After the second bridge, cross onto the pavement to follow the road around to the right. The castle soon comes into view ahead. Cross again and enter through the old gatehouse, noting the route of the footpath down the steps to the right.

4 Leaving the castle, take those steps into the valley. At the bottom, turn left. The route continues with a stream on your right (not always next to the path) for 1.3km (¾ mile), along paths that can get muddy in places.

RIGHT The path between Points 3 and 4.

BELOW The path between Points 1 and 2.

166 FARLEIGH HUNGERFORD CASTLE

Cross the minor road, continuing straight ahead. After some time, the path rises briefly into some woods that are full of spring bulbs. On leaving the woods, you are high above the river. Cross a small field towards some houses.

5 **Turn left onto the tarmac drive, then right after a few metres over a stream and up some steps, with a hedge on your right.** Continue ahead through a gate onto a bridleway into a wood. The river is down to the right. Eventually, the path reaches Middle House. Turn right onto the lane, then right at the road junction. Follow this lane across the river. Where the lane bends right, follow it for about another 50m (55yds). Head left through a gate and across the field, on a clear path. When you reach the road, turn left for a while and then right onto a footpath immediately before the bridge. Join here if you're travelling by train to Freshford station.

6 **Follow the riverside path for 1.5km (1 mile), until you reach a large stone wall.** Continue ahead, then bear right past steps up to the aqueduct. The car park is just beyond the café on the right.

39 FRAMLINGHAM CASTLE

Henry I granted Framlingham to Roger Bigod I in 1101. Roger likely built a timber fort, and his second son, Hugh, started to build the stone castle around 1154 after gaining favour from Henry II for helping him to the throne. However, his ambitions led to a falling-out with Henry II, who confiscated all of Hugh's castles and built one of his own nearby to assert royal power in the area (see Orford Castle, Walk 51).

Framlingham Castle has been home to both ends of the social spectrum during its lifetime. While Mary Tudor was battling for the right to become queen, she was in danger and spent some time in Framlingham, building support for her cause. She was still living in the castle when she heard that her claim had been accepted and she was now Queen Mary.

At the other end of the social scale, in the 17th century the castle's owner bequeathed his lands to his former college on the condition that the castle would be used to shelter the poor. After much legal wrangling, a workhouse was opened within the castle, where destitute people were forced to work to pay for their keep. This poor house operated until 1839.

BELOW Framlingham Castle from the mere.

WALK DETAILS

START/FINISH
Framlingham Castle car park, IP13 9BP

DISTANCE
7km (4⅓ miles)

PARKING
At start, car parks in Framlingham, limited on-street parking

PUBLIC TRANSPORT
Bus from Ipswich or Wickham Market to castle

REFRESHMENTS
Pubs and cafés in Framlingham

TOILETS
In castle (inside entry gate) and in town

THE WALK
An easy walk out across flat arable farmland and back around The Mere. Due to a lack of landmarks and some indistinct paths across the farmland, we recommend downloading the GPX file and having this available in case you find the route difficult to follow.

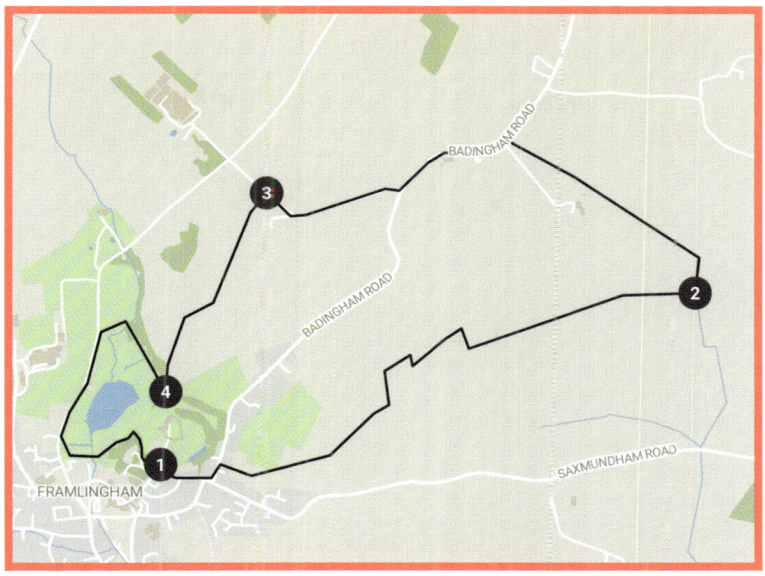

1 **From the castle car park, turn right towards the town then left along the one-way street.** At the end of the road, turn left onto Badingham Road. After a short distance, turn right into Pageant Field. Take the path from the far-left corner over a small wooden bridge and into a field. Head along the left-hand edge of the allotments in the middle of the field. At the end of the allotments, turn left between fields.

At a T-junction of paths near a waymarker, turn left and follow this path as it turns to the right, right again, then left. At the next junction, ignore the path on the left and continue ahead. The path then bends to the right, towards the water tower. After a short distance, it bends left, following the line of the hedge. When the hedge bends to the left, continue straight ahead across the field towards the left side of the small group of trees ahead. Continue past the trees in the same direction. This path eventually leads to a ditch with a waymark post.

2 **Turn left in front of the ditch, and about 100m (110yds) further along, turn left again past a solitary oak tree.** This path skirts a small woodland on the left, and then finishes at a lane. The last few metres of the path can become overgrown. Turn left past Shawsgate Vineyard. Pass some houses on the left, then take the first road on the right. After about 500m (⅓ mile), the road bends to the right and dips into a valley ahead.

3 **Turn left down the footpath. There is a hedge on the left and the land slopes down to the right.**

You will soon get your first glimpse of the castle ahead. The land north and west of the castle used to be the castle's great park. It was primarily for deer and other game, with a fence all around to stop the deer from escaping – and poachers from getting in.

Where the path bends to the left, turn right to follow a line of trees and then a hedge on your left. The castle is now on your left. This path eventually bends left under some trees and splits.

4 Turn right, then right again. The Mere is now visible to your left.

> *The Mere provided food for the castle's household including swans, geese and other waterfowl and their eggs, as well as fish. A dovecot was also sited somewhere in The Mere, providing both meat and eggs. The lake is around 3,000 years old, so it was here well before the castle.*

Just before the playing fields, turn left. Walk a little further, then cross the wooden bridge, pass through the kissing gate and continue on the well-defined path with trees on your right, open marsh on your left and a view to the church.

As you progress on this path, the castle comes back into view on the far side of The Mere. On a still day, the reflections make the castle look even more impressive. The flat piece of land in front of the castle used to be the castle gardens.

Follow this path around The Mere until you're close to the castle. You will have passed two exits. At the third exit, take a path uphill with the castle on your left. When you reach the moat, turn right. This path takes you to the edge of the town. Turn left at the Castle Inn for the entrance to the castle and to return to the car park.

TOP LEFT A section of the route between Points 1 and 2.

ABOVE A view across the fields between Points 1 and 2.

BELOW The castle from the far side of the mere between Point 4 and the end of the walk.

40 GLAMIS CASTLE

Its towers, turrets and surrounding trees place Glamis as one of the finest castle mansions in Scotland. Since the first structure was built, it has had royal connections. Initially, it was a defendable royal hunting lodge, hence its position in a valley. More recently, it was where the Queen Mother grew up and Princess Margaret was born.

This explains, in part at least, the sumptuousness of the rooms and their contents. The castle's walls are 2.5m (8ft) thick, allowing space for some oddities within them, such as the powder room. This is where the men of the house would powder their wigs, adding arsenic to the mix to kill bugs!

George VI's study and dressing room houses the Kinghorne bed from the 17th century. It is a very short bed, made when sleeping horizontally was thought to signify death and giving the Devil a chance to take you early.

The crypt below the tower is where visitors were received, including royalty. The same tower is home to the original well, used as a hiding place for precious items. This suggests that Glamis Castle did see turbulent times, even though it was never attacked by cannon.

WALK DETAILS

START/FINISH
Glamis car park, DD8 1RG

DISTANCE
6.75km (4¼ miles)

PARKING
At start

PUBLIC TRANSPORT
Bus from Dundee or Forfar to Glamis Primary School

REFRESHMENTS
Café in castle (after entry gate)

TOILETS
In castle (after entry gate)

BELOW Glamis Castle as seen from the far end of the avenue at Point 5.

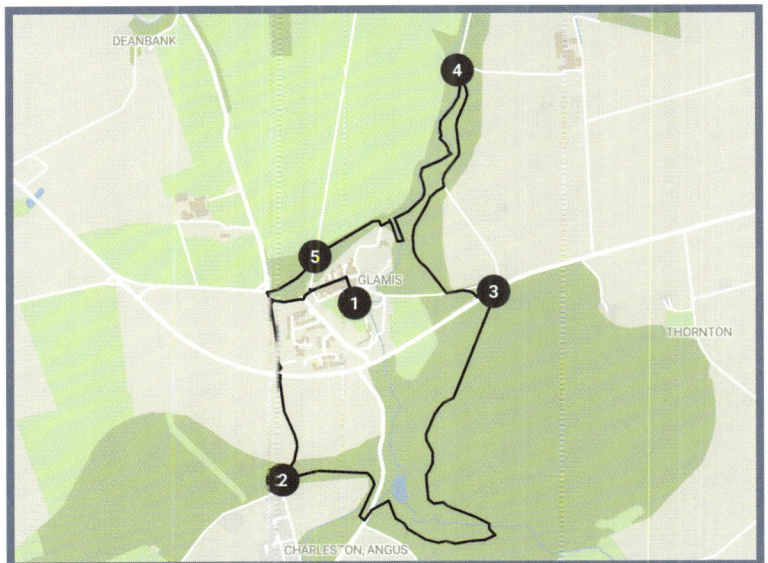

The Walk
A delightful walk, mainly through mixed woodland alongside a babbling stream. Specimen trees combine with native broadleaves and rhododendrons to make an interesting landscape. A view of the castle emerges at the end of the walk, along an impressive oak avenue. Can get boggy in places. Gates open 6am to 6pm.

1 **Return to Main Street along the entrance road to the car park.** At the Strathmore Arms, turn left. Pass the castle gates on your right, and turn right at the junction to continue in the same direction, now with the estate wall on your right. Turn left at the war memorial, onto Charleston Road. At the end of the road, kink right then left on the footpath to meet the A-road. Cross and take the minor road ahead uphill until the Charleston village sign is in sight.

2 **Just before you reach the sign, turn left on the track that passes a house on the right and then heads into woodland, where it becomes a narrow but distinct footpath.** After a while, this path bends around to the right and crosses a stream. Continue ahead after the bridge up to the road. Turn left past the parking space and take the footpath behind the crash barrier on the right, again into the woods. The stream is on your left. At the corner of the fence, turn right along it, with a slope leading down on the left. When this path meets a track at a T-junction, turn sharp left downhill and cross the stream on a bridge. Continue along the track, with the stream on your left. At the next junction of tracks, continue ahead, gently uphill, and stay left as the track flattens off. This track eventually reaches the A-road.

3 **Turn left onto the road for about 30m (33yds), then right down the side road, past the no entry signs.** You'll soon see a wide gate on your right. Turn right down this track. After about 200m (220yds), stay on the path as it gently bends to the right. You can now hear the stream again on your left, although it is not visible. When you meet another track, turn left.

This is a mixed woodland, with native broadleaf trees, intermingled with exotic conifers. There are trees of varying ages, including some impressive specimens.

Eventually, the path reaches the level of the stream.

4 Turn sharp left onto the streamside path. You are now walking upstream, with the stream on your right. Cross two wooden footbridges in quick succession. After some time, cross again at the next bridge and turn right along the wall. Where the path rises up steps to the left, continue ahead for a few metres to St Fergus's Well.

This is where Christians were once baptised, and it is believed that St Fergus lived in the cave behind the well, which has since been infilled.

5 Return to the steps and take them uphill. At the top of the steps, turn right on the drive and follow it around to the left. This drive takes you to the end of the avenue that leads to the castle.

Look right for a distant view of the castle, or turn right to visit the castle. The broad avenue is 1.6km (1 mile) long, and is bordered by oak trees planted in the 17th century. It is said that oak trees grow for 300 years, live for 300 years and die for 300 years. By this reckoning,

174 GLAMIS CASTLE

this avenue should be around for centuries to come. Although used here decoratively, these oak trees are also providing a valuable habitat for wildlife. Some 2,300 species are supported by oak trees, and of those, 326 rely on oak trees to survive.

Facing away from the castle, fork to the right. Exit through the gates and turn left to retrace your steps to the start.

RIGHT The caste gates at Kirkwynd close to the end of the walk – open from 6am to 6pm.

LEFT The path through the woods between Points 3 and 4.

BELOW St Fergus's Well between Points 4 and 5.

41 GOODRICH CASTLE

Goodrich Castle sits on a rocky spur high above the River Wye, on the site of an Iron Age hill fort, with commanding views along the valley. It is named after the Anglo-Saxon Godric Mappeson, who owned an estate here when the Domesday Book was compiled shortly after the Norman Conquest. A few decades later, the land was in the hands of the Normans, who built the stone keep in the middle of the 12th century. The wider defences you can see today, built from a different stone, were erected from the early 13th century to the end of the 14th century and included elaborate apartments. The castle had become a baronial palace as well as a fortification, and this is reflected in the quality of the decorative stonework.

The castle remained untested until 1646, when it was attacked by Parliamentarians in the British Civil Wars and fell to a combination of arson and mortar bombardment.

The chapel is located in the main tower of the gatehouse. It features a slit window to help defend the castle entrance and a socket in the wall to hold the drawbar for the main gate. A small stained-glass window was added in 1992 to commemorate the Radar Research Squadron, and a

WALK DETAILS

START/FINISH
Goodrich Village Hall, HR9 6HX

DISTANCE
8.5km (5¼ miles)

PARKING
On road at start

PUBLIC TRANSPORT
Bus from Gloucester to Cross Keys, 1.25km (¾ mile) walk to start

REFRESHMENTS
Café at castle – near start

TOILETS
At castle (before entry gate)

LEFT The pale Norman keep within red sandstone outer defences.

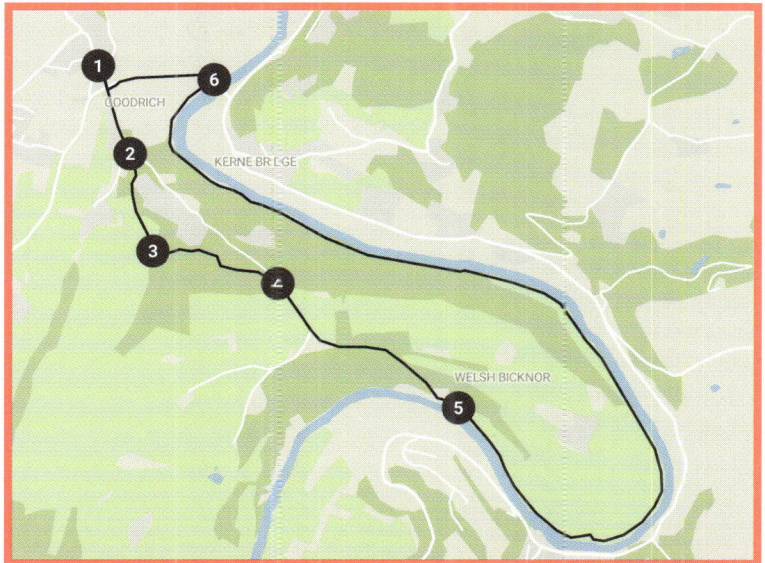

larger one was added in 2000 to celebrate the Millennium.

THE WALK

A climb takes you to the top of Coppett Hill, with far-reaching views over Herefordshire, dropping to the rugged but more intimate grandeur of the Wye Valley. The path by the river is narrow and can get overgrown and muddy in places. Long trousers and waterproof footwear are recommended. One stile.

1 From the village hall, take the road downhill. Fork left past the entrance to the castle car park. Follow this quiet tarmac lane for around 500m (⅓ mile) to a junction of roads.

2 Take the steps uphill into Coppett Hill Common Local Nature Reserve. Follow the path as it zigzags up and around the hill. At the top of a short

BELOW The trig point on Coppett Hill at Point 3.

GOODRICH CASTLE   177

set of steps, turn to the right onto a path heading around the hill.

The valley is now on your right and before long a big view opens up across farmland and Goodrich village.

Eventually, the path leaves the wooded area and continues uphill to the trig point.

From here, there are extensive views to the north and west.

After the Norman invasion, Coppett Hill became the property of the Norman Lord of the manor, along with Goodrich Castle. Those living nearby, known as commoners, would have been Welsh-speaking and had the right to graze animals, forage for food and conduct recreational activities on the land. During the 18th and 19th centuries, much common land in Britain was 'enclosed', and the commoners had their rights revoked. This led to starvation and much unrest, but the commons on Coppett Hill were never enclosed, and commoners' rights continue to this day.

3 From the trig point, fork left into the woods, then between some earthworks on your left and a wall to your right. This path slowly drops, exits the woods for a short period as it crosses the top of a lime kiln, before heading back into the woods and down to a lane. Look to your right to see an old limestone quarry that would have been used for the lime kiln.

4 Turn right along the lane into the Courtfield Estate. Continue down an avenue of oak trees, then bear left through a gate by a cattle grid. After Primrose Cottage, fork right, then right again towards the youth hostel. After 250m (275yds), take the footpath that leads diagonally down to the right of the drive, with the valley to your right, until you reach the river. At the bottom of the path, turn left onto another path that joins a drive between the youth hostel and the river.

You will soon pass St Margaret's Church, built by the Victorians on an ancient site and listed because of the quality of its features. The unusual cross in the churchyard is also Victorian but has some medieval stonemasonry in its base.

5 Follow the path along the side of the river with the water on your right to Kerne Bridge, about 6km (3¾ miles).

This lovely bridge dates from 1828. Although parts of the Forest of Dean are ancient woodland, at that time it was also an industrial area with many coal and iron ore mines. The bridge was built as part of the road used to transport these resources from the forest to South Wales.

From here, there is an optional extension of the walk, continuing along the river and returning to the bridge. All around the left-hand bend of the river, there are views up to the castle on the left.

6 Once you reach the bridge, turn left onto the road.

The beautiful building on the right is Flanesford Priory, built for Augustinian priests in the 14th century. It was one of the first monasteries to fall during the

Reformation and was used as farm buildings before being converted into a holiday let.

TOP Kerne Bridge at Point 6.

ABOVE The path along the river between Points 5 and 6.

Follow the footpath up the road, bearing left as it rises up to a bridge. At the top, turn right to complete the walk.

GOODRICH CASTLE

42 GYLEN CASTLE

Gylen Castle was previously known as Duncan's Fort because it was built by Duncan MacDougall of Dunollie. It is one of a ring of castles, all historically owned by Clan MacDougall.

Gylen Castle was built in 1582 in the Scots baronial style – part home, part castle, with gun loops and pistol holes, a heavy door and an iron grille. The oriel window high above the entrance is both decorative and deadly. It had a floor that was easy to remove so that stones and boiling water could be poured down upon unwanted visitors.

The castle has strong defences; but it was its water supply that was its undoing. With a Royalist garrison inside, it was besieged during the Covenanting Wars (the Covenanters argued that church leaders should be in charge of religious affairs rather than the king). When the castle's defenders capitulated, there was still food inside, so it is thought to have been a lack of water that facilitated the surrender. The occupants were massacred as they left. Only the young John MacDougall, the 19th chief of the clan, survived.

After this final siege, the castle was ransacked and razed so it could not be used again.

WALK DETAILS

START/FINISH
Kerrera Jetty

DISTANCE
11.5km (7¼ miles)

PARKING
At Gallanach ferry terminal, PA34 4QH

PUBLIC TRANSPORT
Train to Oban, then bus to Kerrera Ferry Terminal

REFRESHMENTS
Tea garden at Point 4 (not always open)

TOILETS
At Point 4

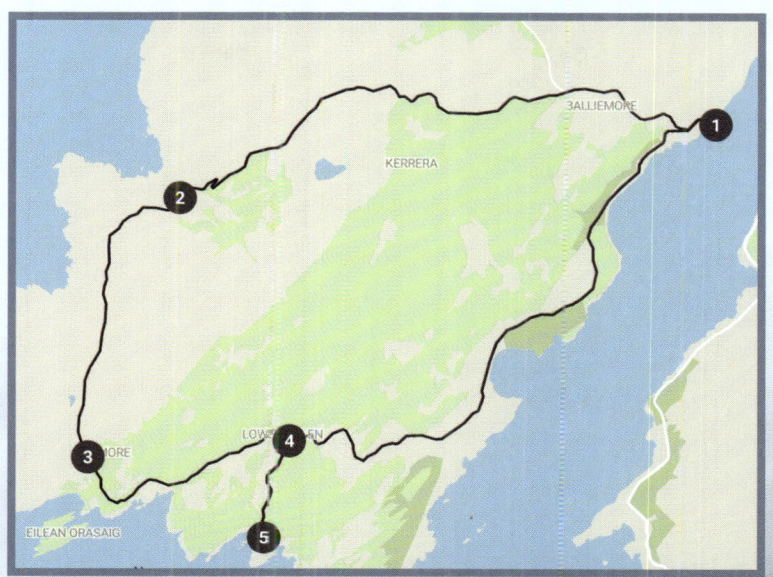

THE WALK

Take the ferry from Gallanach, a short journey south of Oban, to start a walk that circumnavigates the Island of Kerrera. A peaceful, gentle walk along stone tracks with occasional muddy stretches and frequent sea views. Gylen Castle perches above a raised beach, grim, strong and staring out to sea.

BELOW Gylen Castle overlooking the Firth of Lorn.

The only motor vehicles on Kerrera belong to the inhabitants, so this is a quiet island, as it is 12 square km (4⅔ square miles) and home to only 68 people, including children. Wildlife to look out for includes otters, deer and eagles. Golden eagles are huge birds, but white-tailed eagles, also known as sea eagles, are even bigger, likened sometimes

LEFT The decorative and potentially deadly entrance to Gylen Castle.

RIGHT The route between Points 2 and 3.

BOTTOM RIGHT The Sound of Kerrera and Oban as seen from the final stretch of the walk.

This was once an old horsebox selling painted pebbles and dusty jars of jam. Things have changed since then, and it sells all manner of artisan food and goods, as well as ice creams and cold drinks.

Where the tarmac runs out, continue along what is now a stony track. Where the track bends to the right, continue ahead through a gate onto another track.

The lighthouse you can see to the right is on the south-western tip of the island of Lismore. The land you can see behind Lismore is the mainland, and the land to the left is the Isle of Mull.

Continue to the white house.

2 Fork left up past the right-hand end of the building and along the track ahead. Over time, the track narrows into a path, which is muddy in places. The path turns inland between steep slopes and rises. It then drops past a house, at which point it becomes a track again. This is Ardmore, and in the time that Gylen Castle was in use, when boats were the main means of transport here, it was a ferry port.

to a flying barn door. Although eagles are protected, several golden eagles are found poisoned on grouse moors every year. Despite this, populations of both types of eagle are growing in the UK.

1 From the ferry terminal, head straight uphill and to the left along the tarmac drive. Where the drive splits, fork right uphill. Pass the old schoolhouse that is now a community centre and then the farm shop.

3 Continue along the track.

Out to sea, you can spot the island of Colonsay, with Jura and Islay to the left. After a little while, look right for your first view of Gylen Castle.

Continue along the track to Kerrera Tea Garden.

4 Pass the tea garden, cross a small stream then head right through a gate and follow the grassy track towards the sea. After a short distance, you will see the castle ahead. Follow the path to the castle. The climb becomes steep as you near it.

Gylen Castle is built on a knoll of conglomerate. The land here was formed by volcanic activity before the Ice Age scoured it into the shapes we see today. Great ice sheets are heavy, so as they melted, the land rose, leaving raised beaches such as the one in front of Gylen Castle. Although Scotland is still rising, global heating is causing sea levels to rise faster, which means that Scotland is now suffering from net sea level rise.

5 Retrace your steps to return to the gate by the tea garden. Turn right onto the track, away from the buildings. Shortly after the next buildings, follow the track around to the left, ignoring the track on the right.

As you round the island, there is a fantastic view along the Sound of Kerrera to Oban.

Follow this drive around the shore until it reaches the ferry jetty.

In 1249, King Alexander II of Scotland died on Kerrera when he attacked Ewan MacDougall for being granted the title of King of the Isles by the Norwegian king. However, he died from a fever, not battle wounds.

43 INVERARAY CASTLE

The first castle was built at Inveraray in the 15th century, a laird's tower surrounded by a small village. When the earls of Argyll were promoted to dukes in the 18th century, the 2nd Duke thought they should have a grander residence and set to work on the castle we see today. A new town was built down by the quay, and all the residents were moved. The house took some time to build; the first duke to live there was the 5th.

At that time, the only practical way to reach the town was by water. With such limited means of communication, it is astonishing that rooms such as the Tapestry Drawing Room were designed to the height of Parisian fashion. A series of tapestries for the walls was commissioned and shipped from France while the house was being built. These are still in situ today, having survived two house fires, one after a hundred years and the other a century later.

The dukes of Argyll are heads of the Clan Campbell, and the strength of the clan was demonstrated after the fire in 1975 when Campbells around the world clubbed together to make the restoration possible.

BELOW The facade of Inveraray Castle.

WALK DETAILS

START/FINISH
Inveraray car park, PA32 8YH

DISTANCE
8.75km (5½ miles)

PARKING
At start

PUBLIC TRANSPORT
Bus from Glasgow, Dunoon, Campbeltown or Oban to Front Street

REFRESHMENTS
Pubs and cafés in Inveraray, café at castle (after entry gate)

TOILETS
On the quay in Inveraray, in the castle (after entry gate)

The Walk
Spot veteran trees in the castle gardens and throughout the steep woodland walk to the lookout tower, Dun Na Cuaiche. A splendid view over the castle and town and along Loch Fyne, Scotland's longest sea loch. Find hidden ruins of farms, kilns, an ice house and revered springs.

1 **Head to the shore and turn left along Main Street South.** Head around the right side of the church and you will see Inveraray Jail on your right. Continue ahead along the main street.

You will soon see Dun Na Cuaiche, the tower on the hill ahead that you are climbing up to.

Turn left at the end of the main street, and then left up the drive to Inveraray Castle. Follow the drive around to the right past the garden entrance to the castle, and to the main entrance.

2 **After the car park, follow the drive to the left and over the bridge.** At the junction on the far side of the bridge, head diagonally right up into the woods to a track along a stretch of meadow. You will return to this point after visiting the tower.

3 **Cross the track. Continue uphill, through a gate and left into some more woods.**

Look out for the enormous exotic trees scattered through the woods, including the giant redwood on the left just before the ruins. The ruins appear to be old farm buildings and a lime kiln, but they are very well built for such structures, with decorative arches.

As the track crests a rise, fork right uphill. The route climbs to the Dun Na Cuaiche tower on the hill.

The tower was built as a watchtower, as it has far-reaching views along the loch. If you walk to the edge of the slope towards the town, you will also get fantastic views over the castle, the town and the surrounding hills.

4 **Drop back to the junction of tracks, then continue to retrace your steps by turning left.** You will eventually pass the ruins. Go through a small gate on the right then down to the track at the bottom of the grassy slope (Point 3). Turn right here. When you reach the

tarmac road, turn right and then bend left to cross the river.

From the bridge, look down on your right to see the old ford. If you visit in late summer or autumn, look further up the river, and you might see salmon leaping up the weirs.

Turn left along the drive in front of the wall. Follow this road for about 600m (⅓ mile).

Just before reaching the buildings on the left, look to your right where there is an old ice house. In the days before refrigeration, ice was brought up from the river and packed into the ice house, so that it could be used to keep food cool during the summer months.

Continue past the buildings. At the crossroads at the end of the next field, turn right. You are now on a path leading directly away from the castle. When you reach the road, cross and continue ahead. After about 500m (550yds), bear right up a grassy path to a spring with a classical stone wellhouse.

This well once supplied the water for Inveraray New Town.

ABOVE The old wellhouse at Point 5.

5 Continue along the path past the spring. When you reach the entrance to the quarry, continue ahead on the track gently downhill. On reaching the lower track, turn left across the track down through an old gate, then alongside a field.

From this path, look left to see Dun Na Cuaiche on the hill, and the hill fort on the next hill behind it.

At the end of the path, cross the track and continue down the hill towards the loch. Where this road bends to the right, turn left down a tarmac drive. This drive returns you to the start.

LEFT The view from Dun Na Cuaiche tower.
BELOW Loch Fyne from the town.

KENILWORTH CASTLE

Kenilworth Castle was built shortly after the Norman invasion in the 11th century, and a huge mere was created to protect it. Around 1210, the mere was extended to 800m (½ mile) long and 150m (165yds) wide. This powered watermills and provided the castle with food as well as offering protection. It was also valued for recreation. Henry V even built a moated manor house on the bank that he boated to for banqueting, known as 'The Pleasance in the Marsh'.

The castle survived a siege for almost six months in 1266. During this siege, the most modern weapons of warfare and the king's army were pitted against those defending the castle, but the castle held. In the end, disease and starvation, rather than a failure of the castle's defences, led the defenders to accept a negotiated settlement.

Queen Elizabeth I gifted the castle to Robert Dudley in the 16th century. He, in turn, created an Italianate garden for her, which has now been recreated. It is believed that the queen considered marrying Robert Dudley, and there is some speculation that they may have been lovers. The garden would certainly have been a wonderful gift, whether from a lover or friend.

WALK DETAILS

START/FINISH
Kenilworth Castle car park, CV8 1NG

DISTANCE
8.25km (5¼ miles)

PARKING
At start, at Point 3, in Kenilworth

PUBLIC TRANSPORT
Train to Kenilworth

REFRESHMENTS
Café in castle (after entry gate), pubs and cafés in Kenilworth, including at Point 3

TOILETS
At castle (before entry gate)

The Walk

An easy walk along well-defined paths over farmland with great views of the castle. Visit the remains of The Pleasance and its moat cross land that would have been under the mere and return along its historic banks, with more excellent castle views. No stiles, some small muddy patches at times.

BELOW The castle as seen from the final part of the walk.

1 Head to the entrance of the car park and down the drive to the road. Turn left. At the green railings, turn right along the side of a stream and through a gate into the park. Follow the path to a wooden bridge and cross a different stream. Continue ahead to the hedge then turn left onto the tarmac footpath. Where this meets another tarmac path, turn right and then almost immediately left along the bottom edge of a parkland meadow. Before reaching the road, turn left over a wooden bridge. Head diagonally left across the grass to explore the remains of the Abbey of St Mary, which was built contemporaneously to the castle.

2 Pass the stone barn with its front door on your right and head through a gap in the stone wall in front of you. Follow the path diagonally right, then bear right up a slight rise before the path reaches the lake. Join the tarmac path uphill to a road. Turn left and follow this road as it meanders gently downhill past some thatched black and white cottages to a junction. Cross to the car park next to the castle wall.

3 Take the footpath at the far end of the car park, with a high wall on your left.

> *You are now in the moat, which was linked to the mere.*

At the gate, fork right to a stone track. Turn left and follow the track for about 100m (110yds). Turn right through the kissing gate, and follow the clear path diagonally left across the field. Look behind for a great view of the castle. At the next field, head diagonally left again. Remain on the same path across the fields until you reach a few trees and a kissing gate. The path then continues with the hedge on the right for a short distance before turning right and crossing another field. Continue to the red brick house.

4 Turn left onto the lane in front of the house (Saddlers Cottage) and follow it for about 1.5km (1 mile), past several houses then take Chase Wood on the left.

5 As the lane bears right, away from the trees, take a track on the left along the outside edge of the woodland. At the end of the woodland, continue straight ahead on the same track. Where a public footpath crosses the track before the next area of woodland, turn left along the left-hand edge of a field. Keep the field boundary to your left for the next field, and then turn left through a kissing gate and walk along the right-hand edge of the next one.

> *The castle comes back into view ahead.*

Through another kissing gate, cross a farm track and continue ahead to the remains of The Pleasance in the Marsh, now a series of mounds in a meadow, with the remnants of the moat still holding water.

6 Follow the path through The Pleasance to a wooden gate in a corner of the field. Turn right onto the track in front of the gate and follow it as it bends left over a cattle grid, crosses a small stream then another cattle grid to the next field boundary. You are now crossing the site of the old mere.

At a cluster of gates at the end of the track, turn left through a kissing gate and cross a series of fields, heading towards the castle and then alongside it. This path is along the old banks of the mere and will return you to the car park.

LEFT The Pleasance at Point 6.

RIGHT The Atlas fountain in the castle garden.

BELOW The track between Points 5 and 6.

45 KILCHURN CASTLE

Kilchurn Castle feels pretty remote now, standing on a boggy peninsula at one end of Loch Awe. However, take a step back in time, and this was a far busier spot. The loch itself was an important thoroughfare. It had several castles along its length, and there was a community here on the Campbells of Glenorchy's estate. The water level of the loch was higher, and the castle would have been more prominent, standing on a rocky outcrop surrounded by water.

In the early 21st century, a conifer plantation was felled on the hills to the south-east of the castle, revealing the presence of some ancient open-grown oaks with fused multiple stems. These suggest that this is the location of the estate's 17th-century hunting park.

The remains of the castle visible today are the tower house from the mid-15th century, as well as barracks and additional defences added in the late 17th century, including the curtain walls with circular towers. The castle was subject to a lightning strike in the 1760s. As the owner at that time wished to devote his attention to his lowland estate, the castle was abandoned.

WALK DETAILS

START/FINISH
St Conan's Kirk, Lochawe PA33 1AQ

DISTANCE
10.25km (6⅓ miles)

PARKING
Lay-by at start

PUBLIC TRANSPORT
Train to Loch Awe (there is a pavement along the A-road to the start of the walk), bus to St Conan's Road Junction

REFRESHMENTS
Café at kirk, pub in Lochawe village

TOILETS
None on route

BELOW Kilchurn Castle from the peninsula (credit: iStock).

RIGHT St Conan's Kirk.

THE WALK

St Conan's provides moody views of Kilchurn Castle. The route climbs above Loch Awe to Cruachar Dam. Easy, moderately steep access all the way to the world's first reversible pumped storage hydro system. Options for descending steps to the dam footings or extending your walk alongside the reservoir.

St Conan's Kirk is unique. Like the castle, it was built by the Campbells and the church contains their family tombs. Built between the 1880s and 1930s, St Conan's Kirk was designed by Walter Douglas Campbell, who picked the bits he liked most from other churches. Some say that he tried to incorporate every

style of architecture found in churches across Scotland. This has resulted in an eclectic mix of styles. On the outside of the church, look up to see the hares used to channel water from the roof, flying buttresses that also act as drains and fern leaf designs built into the stonework of one of the towers.

A Celtic-style cross stands proudly in front of the church. From here, you can see the cloisters and their lead roof decorated with an arts and crafts grapevine pattern. The cloisters were purely built for show; they serve no purpose. Spot the narrow stone steps that lead up from nowhere around the tower, stonework from a Glaswegian church that was demolished and a couple of mortsafes leaning against the wall.

Norman-style arches lead into the church, and inside there are carved wooden choir stalls. A simple wooden altar stands in the middle of an apse reminiscent of an elvish hall from Tolkien films. This unusual church is well worth a visit.

1 From St Conan's Kirk, head uphill for a short distance and turn right onto St Conan's Road. Follow this road as it heads uphill (ignore early turn-offs to houses), all the way to the dam at Ben Cruachan. Cross to the far side of the dam.

Shortly after leaving the village, look for woodland below the track. It is what remains of

ancient wood pasture. Further south, there is a large area of old oak coppice interspersed with charcoal platforms. When cut down (coppiced), oak trees shoot up multiple stems, which can be harvested every decade or so. Charcoal is created by slow-burning logs with very little oxygen. This concentrates the calorific value, so charcoal burns hotter than wood. In the 18th and 19th centuries, this charcoal would have been used in local iron furnaces.

2 Return the way you came.

To extend the walk, take the track on the far side of the dam around the reservoir and return when you are ready. (It is possible to walk around the whole of the lake, but there is no path from the end of the track, the ground is boggy and there are streams to ford. It's hard going – and potentially dangerous in places.)

If you would like to see the dam from the bottom, take the stairs down from the top of the dam, follow the footpath with steps down to the track, then follow the track back to St Conan's Road (this route is visible in its entirety from the top of the dam, except, perhaps, on the foggiest of days).

The dam on Ben Cruachan is only part of Cruachan power station. A kilometre-long (²⁄₃ mile) tunnel runs inside the granite mountain, which houses the electricity-generating turbines and is impressive to visit. Cruachan was the first reversible pumped storage hydro power station of this scale in the world. It is now coming into its own, supporting the transition to renewables by dropping water through the turbines to create power when demand outstrips supply and pumping it back up when there is spare capacity in the grid.

LEFT The dam at Ben Cruachan.
BELOW The castle from across Loch Awe to the south (credit: Swen Stroop/Shutterstock).

46 LANCASTER CASTLE

In a familiar story of succession, Lancaster Castle was built by the Normans on the site of an old Roman fort that itself was built on the site of an old Iron Age fort. Lancaster is now well within England's borders, but these were contested lands for centuries. After their conquest, the Normans built a wooden fortress here, soon replaced by a stone keep surrounded by curtain walls, towers and ditches.

Norman castles were often used as courts and prisons, and Lancaster is no exception. The Crown Court still meets here, and the castle was used as a prison into the 21st century. In the 19th century, Lancaster was often used as a debtors' prison. The wealthier debtors paid for a more comfortable cell and even employed some of the poorer debtors as servants. During this period, Lancaster was England's second most prolific hanging court. However, it was notorious for its hangings well before that. In 1612, the Lancashire Witches were tried here.

WALK DETAILS

START/FINISH
Lancaster railway station, LA1 5NW

DISTANCE
9km (5½ miles)

PARKING
Car parks near castle and station, Lune Aqueduct car park LA1 3UA (join just after Point 3)

PUBLIC TRANSPORT
Train or bus to Lancaster railway station

REFRESHMENTS
Café shortly after leaving the canal and at the Ashton Memorial

TOILETS
At castle (free entry)

BELOW Lancaster Castle gatehouse.

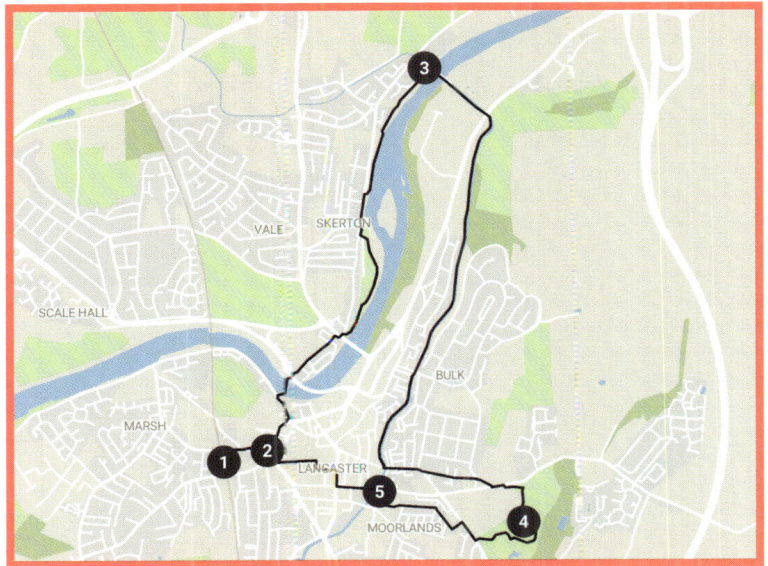

With hindsight, it seems the Catholic powers were trying to curry favour with the Protestant king. Ten people were condemned and hanged – the largest single execution of witches in England's history.

THE WALK
From the train to the castle in just a few steps. Contrast the noise of the city with the peaceful but spectacular Skerton Weir on the River Lune. Views from the Lune Aqueduct, a relaxed canal-side walk and a short climb lead to panoramas from Williamson Park over the city and beyond.

1 Leave the station by the booking office and turn left up a footpath. At the end, turn right uphill to the castle, which is on the left.

2 Turn left around the far side (front) of the castle, then down Castle Hill. This takes you down to the Judges' Lodgings Museum.

BELOW The view from the footbridge over the River Lune between Points 2 and 3.

LANCASTER CASTLE

This is where the judges who came to the court in the castle stayed when visiting.

Continue down to the modern road and turn left, then take the first left along Damside Street. Pass the memorial to the horrors of the slave trade, then cross the modern footbridge over the river. Cross under the road, and then go along a residential street ahead. At the end, cross the busy road and turn down towards the river, walking along it with the water on your right. At the end of the tarmac path, turn right onto a minor road. Turn right immediately past the rowing club, and you will see the unusual weir construction, marking the end of the tidal river.

Further upstream, the Lune Aqueduct is now also visible.

Continue upstream until you reach the jetty. Turn up the steps and continue in the same direction. At a junction of paths, turn right and down some steps, still upstream, to the aqueduct.

3 **Stay high and turn right to cross it.** Look to the right for a view over the castle.

Follow the canal for some distance back into the city. Eventually, you will pass a warehouse. Turn up the steps and cross the next bridge – number 102 – then continue ahead, gently uphill. At the fork in the road, keep left. At the top of the road, continue uphill into an alley. Cross the next road, climb a small flight of steps, and cross the grass to another small flight of steps. Turn left at the road, then right through stone gateposts and left uphill. At the top of the path, turn right onto the wide tarmac path, towards the Ashton Memorial.

The big concrete blocks on the coast to your right are Heysham nuclear power station. There is also a great view of the castle from here, which reveals its strategic position on the only hill in the town.

Find your way up to the memorial, and up inside it if allowed/desired. Behind the memorial is a butterfly house and café, and a pebble mosaic.

4 **Facing downhill with your back to the memorial, turn left to pass between two magnificent copper beeches (with purple leaves).** Turn sharp right immediately after the beech trees onto a path that winds its way down through the woodland to a road. Turn right. Take the second left down Ayr Street, then turn right at the end down Kirkes Road. At the T-junction, cross onto Balmoral Road, continuing downhill towards the cathedral. Turn right at the end and the entrance to the Catholic cathedral is a little further along on your right.

LEFT The Ashton Memorial at Point 4.

ABOVE The canal between Points 3 and 4.

5 The route continues past the cathedral and turns left over the canal past the Town Hall to Dalton Square. Turn right, then take the first left onto Gage Street. Continue ahead along the alley where the road bends left, and then turn right onto the pedestrian street. At the crossroads, turn left onto Market Street. Continue past the market hall and cross the road at the end of the pedestrian precinct. Then take the first right, Castle Hill, to the castle. To return to the station, turn left in front of the castle then descend on Castle Park.

47 LEEDS CASTLE

Leeds is a beautiful castle surrounded by wide, attractive moats and has primarily acted as a royal residence and country house rather than a fortification.

It was once attacked, though, by Isabella of France, Edward II's queen consort. In 1321, Lord Badlesmere, the castle's owner, was becoming rebellious. It seems that Isabella requested hospitality on a pilgrimage to Canterbury to bring things to a head and was turned away by Lady Badlesmere. Consequently, the queen consort's small army attacked the castle. In retaliation, Lady Badlesmere instructed her archers to attack the queen consort's men. Six died. The king declared this as an act of treason. The castle was besieged for two weeks, and the Badlesmeres finally capitulated. Lady Badlesmere and her children were imprisoned in the Tower of London, and Lord Badlesmere was beheaded. That's one way to deal with people who disagree with you!

The tour of the castle itself focuses on the living quarters of Lady Baillie,

WALK DETAILS

START/FINISH
Leeds Castle Gatehouse, Broomfield, ME17 1RG

DISTANCE
9.5km (6 miles)

PARKING
At castle (add another 1.6km (1 mile) to your walk) or Broomfield Road, Kingswood (Point 3)

PUBLIC TRANSPORT
Train to Hollingbourne railway station then a 3km (1¾ miles) walk to the castle

REFRESHMENTS
Café in castle (after entry gate), pub in Leeds

TOILETS
At castle (before entry gate)

BELOW Leeds Castle and its moat.

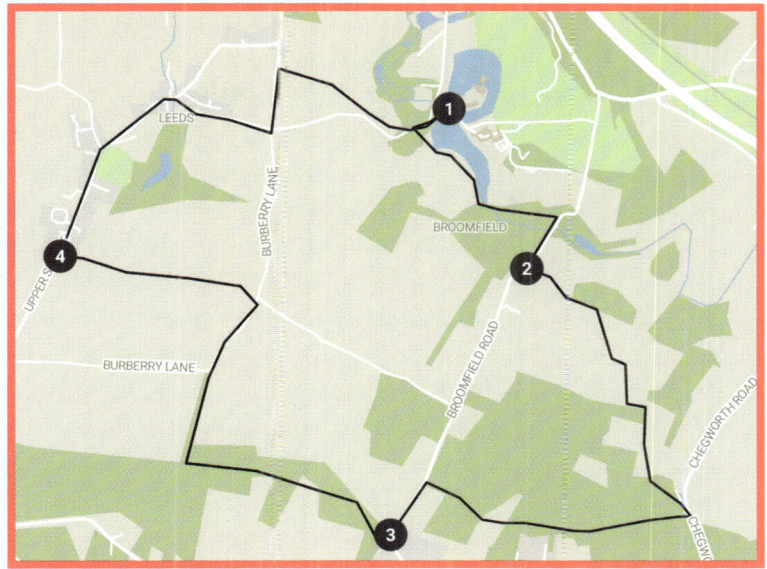

an Anglo-American heiress who bought and renovated the castle in the 1920s. The castle is very much run as a visitor attraction with gardens, a maze, birds of prey and activities to keep children entertained.

THE WALK

The rolling hills of Kent provide the perfect backdrop for this lovely walk through coppiced woodlands and over green fields, punctuated by the jewel that is Leeds Castle, sitting proudly on its island in the middle of a wide moat. This is easy walking through beautiful countryside.

ABOVE Welcome to Leeds village, towards the end of the walk.

1 **For an excellent view of the castle reflected in the moat, follow the path with the moat on your left.** This is a public footpath: other parts of the castle grounds are only accessible with a ticket.

Return to the gatehouse, turn your back to it and walk ahead. Turn left on the far side of the lake and follow the public footpath with the lake on your left. At the far end, the path enters

a woodland. There is a small muddy section here. Where the path reaches a road, turn right and stay on the road for 250m (275yds) until you reach the church entrance and Broomfield village sign.

2 **Turn left and follow the public footpath through the churchyard.**
On leaving the churchyard, continue ahead to a copse. Continue with the trees on your left until you reach the hedgerow. Pass through the gate and follow the path diagonally to the far corner of the field ahead.

When you reach the woodland, turn left and then right, keeping the woodland on your right.

Follow the path as it bends to the left, cutting off the corner of the field. Continue on the path into the woodland ahead for a few metres, before turning left onto the track that runs past a house on the left. About 20m (65ft) before the track reaches a road, take the footpath on the right heading back into the woods. At the confluence of paths by a tall oak, keep to the right of the tree and continue straight ahead. You will know you have chosen the right path if you soon see some houses on the far side of a paddock on the left.

> This area is coppiced. The continuous cycle of cutting trees down, allowing light and warmth to the forest floor, creates a habitat for diverse ground flora and lengthens the trees' lifespan.

This path continues through the woodland for around 1km (⅔ mile) until it reaches another road. Once there, turn left and follow the road until it bears left.

3 Turn right immediately before the first garden on the right, then immediately right, away from the garden fence. This path leads through a coppiced woodland, which is carpeted in bluebells in spring. Where the path forks right into a field, stay left among the trees. At the next junction of paths, continue ahead. Eventually, you will reach a junction of paths with a field a few metres in front of you. Turn right here along a wide path through the trees to a tarmac lane.

Turn right towards the ridge in the distance. After 400m (440yds), at a junction with another road, turn diagonally left across an arable field. Cross under the electricity lines, then turn left to follow them. Two-thirds of the way across the field, the path bends slightly to the right of the power lines, and reaches a busy B-road.

4 Cross the road and turn right onto the pavement. This path will take you down into the village of Leeds to the George pub. Turn right onto the lane immediately before the pub and follow this to a crossroads. Turn left and follow this for about 150m (165yds). Pass a converted oast house, then a beautiful old stone house to a junction of paths. Turn right onto the Len Valley Walk, heading directly away from the road. Continue in more or less the same direction, looking left for a view of the castle, until you reach a drive. Turn left towards the castle and continue to the gatehouse.

LEFT The woodland path between Points 3 and 4.

BELOW Leeds Castle in its woodland setting, as seen from the final leg of the walk.

LINCOLN CASTLE

Lincoln Castle is unique for a couple of reasons.

First is the Magna Carta. This charter restricted the king's power in favour of the barons but still included punitive clauses related to hunting in the royal forests. The Charter of the Forest relaxed these clauses to give some rights to commoners too. These two documents together mark the beginning of the rights and freedoms that everyday citizens enjoy in Britain today. Lincoln Castle is the only place that has original copies of both documents on display.

Second is the prison chapel. It was built when criminality was thought to be contagious, and criminals should, therefore, be kept in isolation. Prisoners were required to attend daily services, so the chapel was designed so that prisoners could not communicate with each other but could still see the chaplain. It is the only example of this style of chapel in the world. The castle still contains a Crown Court but, hopefully, prisoners are treated with greater humanity now.

The Romans were the first to build a fortification here. Lincoln became one of their four provincial capitals, and when the Normans arrived, they built this castle on the same site.

THE WALK

This walk starts and ends at the castle, on the top of an escarpment. It drops down to West Common, a parkland and meadow grazed by horses. You return to the city along the canal, then climb back to the castle and cathedral via the notorious Steep Hill.

BELOW The old prison inside the castle walls (credit: Durden Images/ Shutterstock).

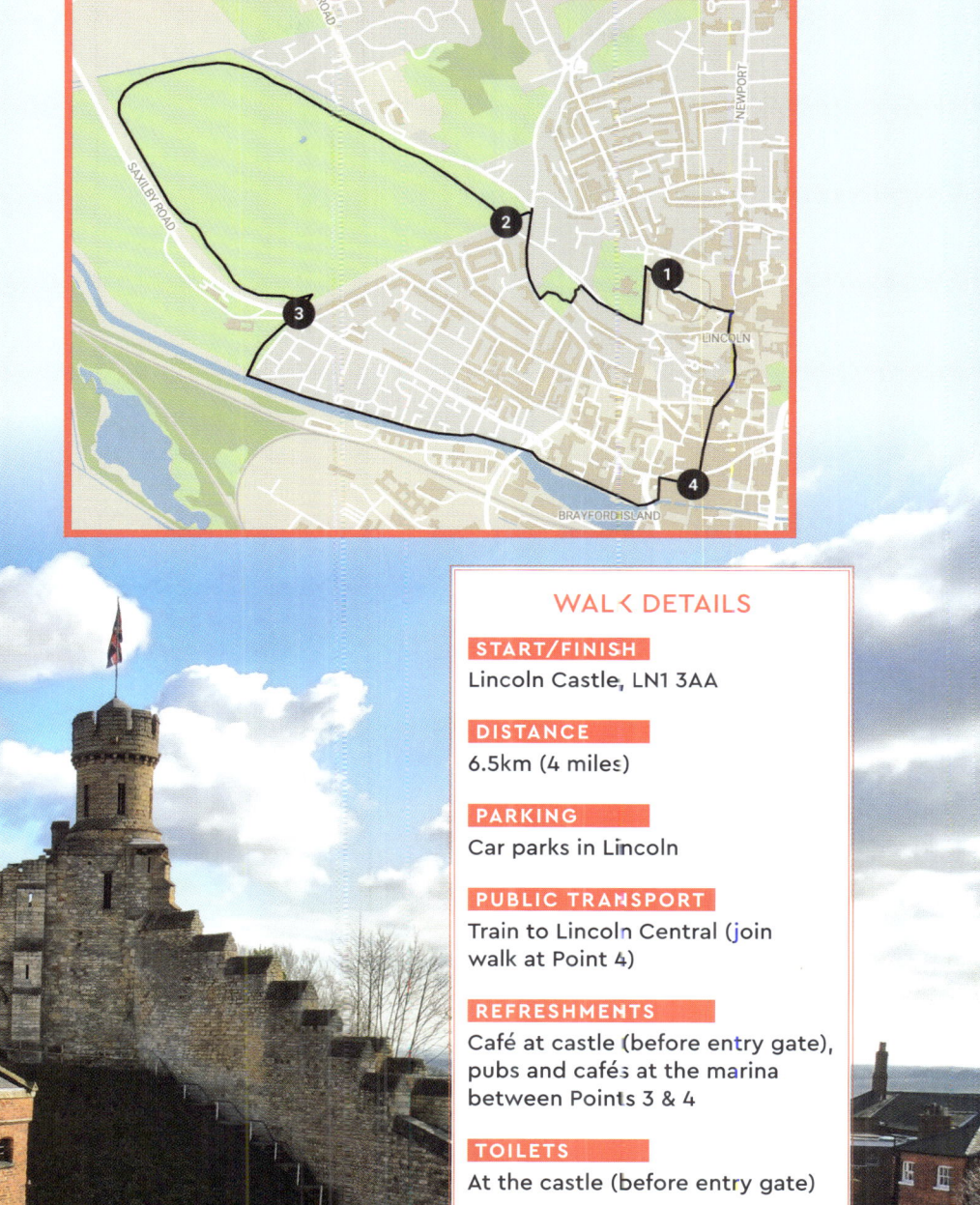

WALK DETAILS

START/FINISH
Lincoln Castle, LN1 3AA

DISTANCE
6.5km (4 miles)

PARKING
Car parks in Lincoln

PUBLIC TRANSPORT
Train to Lincoln Central (join walk at Point 4)

REFRESHMENTS
Café at castle (before entry gate), pubs and cafés at the marina between Points 3 & 4

TOILETS
At the castle (before entry gate)

1 From the western exit of the castle, walk to the road and turn left. At the end of the road, turn right onto Carline Road. After a short distance, take the left fork. Turn left into Liquorice Park Millennium Green, down a flight of steps. Make your way to the far corner of the park, exiting at Yarborough Road. Turn right and walk as far as the pedestrian crossing. Cross here, then head through the gap in the wooden fence. The path follows the back gardens for a while, then you'll see the park open up to your right.

2 Take the first gate into the park and walk directly ahead towards a line of trees to the left of a red brick house. The route follows three sides of the park, but you are of course free to explore at will.

> This is West Common, open land that commoners have had grazing rights on since the mid-16th century, and which is still grazed by horses under the more modern rights. In WWI, the common had two runways and aircraft hangars, and was used as an aircraft test centre for the engineering companies based in Lincoln.
>
> As you reach the final side of the park, look left for a view of the old city, including the windmill, water tower, cathedral and, on the far-right side of the hill, the castle. The castle is dwarfed by the cathedral, which held the title of the world's tallest building for 200 years.
>
> The windmill is the last of the nine that once adorned the ridge. Ellis Mill was built in 1798 and remains in use, grinding flour. It is owned by the council and they sometimes hold open days.
>
> The water tower was built in 1911 and designed to look grand, in line with the city's historic buildings.
>
> Horse racing came to West Common in the late 18th century and the first grandstand was built in the

LEFT Steep Hill on the final leg of the walk.

RIGHT Boats moored on the Fossdyke Navigation canal between Points 3 and 4.

BELOW West Common between Points 2 and 3.

19th century, replaced by the current one in 1897.

Pass the tennis courts, then turn sharp right to the road.

3 Cross the road and take the footpath straight ahead, alongside the golf course to the canal. Turn left along the bank and continue along the canal into the city and past the marina.

The marina is known as Brayford Pool and was once very different to the recreational area we see now. Imagine warehouses and mills clamouring for space to access the water, an important means of transport.

Pass the Royal William IV pub and continue with the water on your right under a low bridge. Then, turn left towards Cathedral Quarter. At the end, turn immediately right along Guildhall Street to the old stone arch.

4 Turn left under the arch. Head uphill along the High Street until it forks. Take the right fork and continue uphill. The cathedral is directly ahead. This road turns into Steep Hill, a name that it lives up to.

At the top, you will see the eastern entrance to the castle on your left and the cathedral to your right.

Construction of Lincoln Cathedral began shortly after the Norman Conquest, at a similar time to the castle. It has faced a great many challenges over the centuries: it has been damaged by fire and earthquake; the central tower collapsed after 150 years; after rebuilding, its central spire was blown down; and the cathedral was damaged during the British Civil Wars. The cathedral hosts two libraries, where visitors can see medieval books over the summer months.

LINCOLN CASTLE

49 MANORBIER CASTLE

Although Manorbier is a defensive castle, it was never attacked as it was built after the Normans had already conquered this part of Wales. It was built for Odo de Barri, a Norman knight who was granted this land in recognition of his role in the conquest. It is easy to imagine living a comfortable life within its walls.

The castle stands on an outcrop in a fertile valley overlooking the sea. This means that there was plenty of food. The sea provided seafood and a means of import and export. The fertile land was suitable for growing crops, boosted by a deer park, fishpond and dovecote for meat and eggs.

The castle's hall is thought to be the earliest stone building in any castle in Wales. During its time, it has seen many Norman nobles and other pilgrims through its doors. In the 12th century, the castle's owner was given special dispensation over the amount he gave to the poor because of the amount he had to spend wining and dining pilgrims. At the time, two pilgrimages to St David's were considered to be the equivalent of one pilgrimage to Rome, so it was a popular route.

WALK DETAILS

START/FINISH
Roadside car park, Manorbier SA70 7SZ

DISTANCE
9.5km (6 miles)

PARKING
At start or Manorbier car park near the castle

PUBLIC TRANSPORT
Train to Manorbier (2km (1¼ miles) from castle), bus to Manorbier House

REFRESHMENTS
Café in castle

TOILETS
In castle (after entry gate) and Manorbier car park

BELOW The castle as seen from the road.

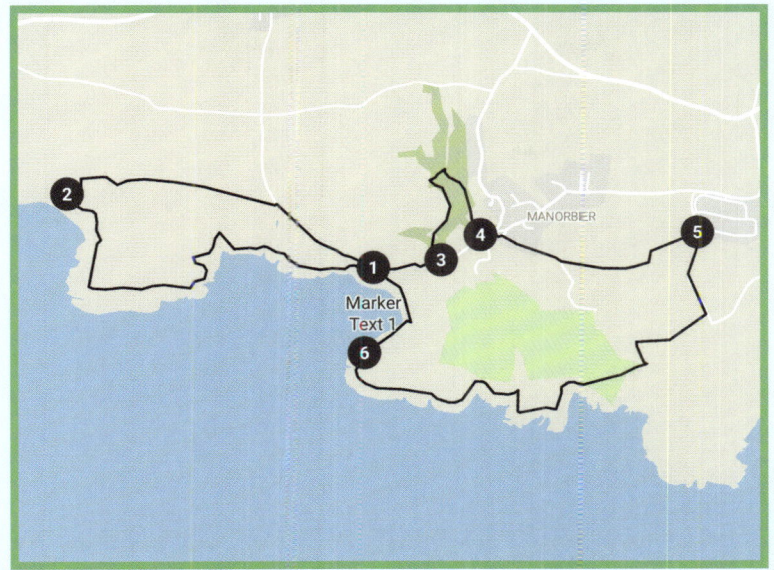

THE WALK

This walk takes in the clifftops of Pembrokeshire and two bays as it follows the Wales Coast Path, then diverts inland to return to Manorbier, circling the castle for the best views and to visit the dovecote. It can easily be split into two circular walks from the car park.

1 From the car park, take the path that runs in front of the benches with the sea to your left. You are on the Wales Coast Path. Follow the path down a drive towards a house and then between the house and the sea. Continue on the coast path for about 2km (1¼ miles) around a headland, and until it reaches the next sandy bay. At the headland, take the clear path up the ridge instead of following the old coast path, which has eroded over the years.

2 At the junction of paths halfway along Swanlake Bay, fork right up the hill. Follow the path as it turns right through a kissing gate next to a stone stile. At the next stone stile and kissing gate, continue straight ahead across the farm track and through a gate. This path passes through several gates and runs between a hedge and a fence until it reaches a minor road. Turn right onto the road and follow it past the car park towards Manorbier. With the National Park car park (and toilets) visible on the right, look for a tarmac lane on the left with a waymarker.

3 Follow signs for the dovecote. Just before reaching it, look right for an impressive view of the castle.

Unusually, you can duck inside the dovecote and see all the ledges for the birds.

The route continues past the dovecote with the castle on your

MANORBIER CASTLE

right. At a fork in the path, bear left, following the waymarker. At the drive for Park Farm, turn right along the drive. After 100m (110yds), just before the cattle grid, turn right onto a path that gently rises through the woods. Ignore the steps up to the left and continue on the same path as it drops, the sound of the stream remaining on your right. Continue ahead as the path leaves the woods and crosses a field. Through the gate, take the path straight ahead, which soon bends to the left through more scrubby woodland to the castle drive.

4 Turn right to visit the castle or left to continue on the route. At the end of the drive, turn right downhill and follow the road around to the left. Take the lane immediately past the entrance to Castle Mead. After 300m (330yds), fork left at a public footpath sign along a track that passes a cottage and then turns into a footpath. Pass a lime kiln on your left. Follow the path as it passes through a gate and turns left uphill before bending back around to the right across a grassy field to some houses.

5 Turn right onto the road. Just before the first buildings of the army base on your right, turn right to follow the acorn waymarkers. You're now back on the Wales Coast Path and the security fence is on your left. Keep the fence on your left as it bends to the left. At the head of the cliffs, pass through the gate and turn right along the clifftop path. Eventually, the path rounds the headland with Manorbier Bay ahead and a fantastic view of the castle. Continue to the stone dolmen.

This is a burial chamber called King's Quoit, from the Stone Age.

6 At this point, keep left and continue along the base of the cliffs onto Manorbier Beach.

If you want to keep your feet dry, cross the stream on the bridge at the top of the beach and continue ahead up some steps to the car park where you started. Alternatively, it's an easy paddle across the stream.

TOP RIGHT Inside the castle walls.
BOTTOM RIGHT The woodland path between Points 3 and 4.
BELOW King's Quoit at Point 6.

50 NORWICH CASTLE

Until recently, the keep at Norwich Castle was an almost empty shell. That was until a £15m project to reinstate all five storeys with their original room layout. Audio-visual displays help to bring the building to life, showing visitors what existence in the castle was like for all the different echelons of society.

A new 18-metre-long (59ft) tapestry, stitched in the same style as the Bayeux Tapestry, updates the story with what happened after the Battle of Hastings. The update starts with the construction of Norwich Castle, which was initially made from timber. At least 98 Anglo-Saxon homes were demolished to make way for the earthworks. When the wooden keep was replaced with a stone one, the materials were imported from Caen in Normandy. It was designed more as a royal palace than a fortification, although it was never used as such.

The tapestry goes on to tell the story of Hereward the Wake, a local hero who led an uprising against the Normans. It also tells of the revolt of the earls and how, as the Earl of East Anglia dashed to Europe to find reinforcements, his 16-year-old wife held the castle against the king's army.

WALK DETAILS

START/FINISH
Norwich railway station, NR1 1EF

DISTANCE
8.75km (5½ miles)

PARKING
At start and Point 3

PUBLIC TRANSPORT
Train or coach to Norwich

REFRESHMENTS
Pubs and cafés in Norwich, café close to Point 4, café between Points 4 & 5

TOILETS
At start and Point 4

BELOW Norwich Castle keep (credit: iStock).

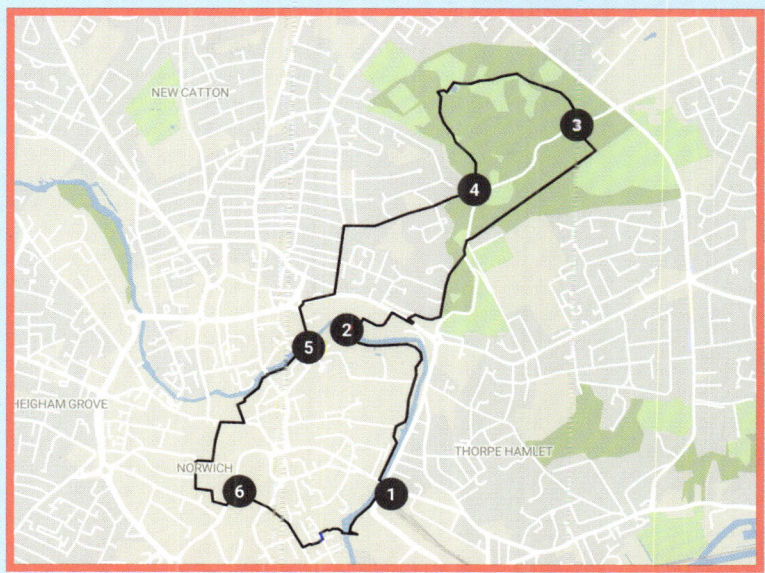

THE WALK

This fairly flat route starts along the river, then rises into woodlands and lowland heath before returning to the river and through the historic city. As there are so many paths across Mousehold Heath, we advise downloading the GPX file for this walk to help with navigation.

1 From the front of the station, head diagonally right across the car park. Cross the road then the river. At the end of the bridge, turn right across a pub terrace onto Riverside Walk. Stay on Riverside Walk as it weaves close to the river and a little further away. Shortly after Cow Tower, you will reach a modern pedestrian bridge.

2 Cross the river. On the far side, walk away from the river and turn right at the far end of Dragonfly House. Stay on the path as it bends left and reaches a road. Turn right, then left on the path that crosses the verge. Turn right onto Cannell

BELOW The view of the river from Point 5.

ABOVE Norwich Guildhall between Points 5 and 6.

RIGHT The woodland path between Points 2 and 3.

Green. At the end, turn left and keep the woodland on your right. Where the road bends to the left with a cobble bank ahead, turn right onto a path into the trees. Fork left almost immediately and follow this path diagonally up to the far side of the woods. At the road, turn left. At the junction ahead, turn diagonally right up a gravel track. Continue straight ahead until you reach a tarmac path crossing this one. Continue ahead on a narrower footpath. After about 200m (220yds), the view opens up to the golf course on your right and lowland heath on your left. Before reaching the trees, take the obvious path to the left just before a drain cover. After about 175m (190yds), you will reach Gurney Road.

3 Cross the road, then the car park, heading in approximately the same direction. Follow this track through the woods as it gradually bends to the left. At a crossroads of paths with a bench and two oak trees, cross then bear left and remain on this path as it heads almost west. When you reach a small pond, turn left with the pond on your left. Fork right just before the trees. After a few metres, at a junction of paths, turn left. Follow this path south and then south-east for about 500m (⅓ mile) to the junction of Gurney Road and Mousehold Avenue.

4 Turn right onto Mousehold Avenue into a residential area. Follow this road to a crossroads. Turn left. The cathedral is directly ahead. At the bottom of this road, turn right, then left at the roundabout. Cross the river.

5 Turn right onto the riverside path. At the first bridge, the path skirts the Ribs of Beef pub before returning to the river. Just before the next bridge, the path again moves away from the river. Follow the path on the left of the red brick wharf building through a courtyard to a pedestrian street. Turn left. At the end, turn right onto St Andrew's Street. After about 100m (110yds), turn left by the pedestrian crossings. On reaching the market square, turn right. After the Guildhall, turn left along the top of the square. Continue past St Peter Mancroft Church. Turn left down the far side of the church, then right at the bottom. Pass the entrance to the Lamb Inn, then take the next left past another entrance. Turn left at the end. The castle is directly ahead. Turn right onto Farmers Avenue. After about 20m (65ft), turn left for access to the castle.

6 To finish the route, continue along Farmers Avenue. At the end of the road, dogleg left then right between Prospect House and Raleigh Court. Take a left down St Julian's Alley, downhill past the church to a road with a half-timbered building ahead. Turn left, then right around the building to the river. Cross the footbridge, then turn left along the riverside to return to the station.

51 ORFORD CASTLE

Today, Orford feels like a sleepy village buzzing with tourists, but when the castle was built, it was a thriving port that rivalled Ipswich. The spit we now know as Orford Ness sheltered the moorings from the sea, but over time the port silted up, and Ipswich became the prominent centre of trade in the area.

The castle was built by Henry II in the late 12th century to help him assert his authority over the local baron, whose castles he had confiscated (see Framlingham Castle, Walk 35). Like most other Norman castles, Orford Castle initially had a curtain wall enclosing a bailey, surrounded by a ditch. The wall was largely dismantled in the 17th century, and subsequent quarrying means the mounds and ditches visible today have nothing to do with the original castle.

WALK DETAILS

START/FINISH
Orford Riverside car park, IP12 2NU

DISTANCE
6.5km (4 miles)

PARKING
At start

PUBLIC TRANSPORT
Bus from Wickham Market to Orford (change at Kelsale)

REFRESHMENTS
Pubs and café in Orford

TOILETS
At start

All that remains is the keep, which was re-rendered in 2022 to replicate what it initially looked like and preserve the tower. The design is unusual – most of Henry II's castles have square or rectangular keeps, but this one is circular with three rectangular turrets. It is thought that this was to show other European powers that he was part of the international elite. It is undoubtedly an impressive piece of architecture.

The Walk
If you enjoy birdwatching, bring your binoculars for this waterfront walk. The first part of the route follows the tidal rivers Ore and Butley, with the return leg crossing arable farmland. Great views across the marsh to the castle and huge skies characterise this flat and easy-to-follow walk.

1 From the entrance to the car park, turn left past the Old Customs House to the quay.

LEFT The keep is all that is left of Orford Castle.
BELOW The route between Points 1 and 2.

Orford thrived after the castle was built here and trade increased. In medieval times, Orford had a church, a friary and two hospitals to service the busy trading port that was close to the mouth of the River Ore. The port is now 8km (5 miles) north of the river mouth, as Orford Ness has lengthened over time.

Turn right along the bank of the River Ore.

The other side of the river is Orford Ness, an internationally important shingle beach that has been owned by the National Trust since 1993. The land used to be owned by the MoD, and during its tenure it was used to test aeroplanes as weapons of war, for research to help develop radar and for bombing trials. It was also used by the Atomic Weapons Research Establishment for a while.

During the Napoleonic Wars of the early 19th century, Britain feared an invasion by France and built a series of Martello towers to protect the vulnerable coastline. Where Orford Ness touches land to the north, the most northerly and largest of these towers still stands.

Because shingle is so mobile, it rarely supports much plant life. On Orford Ness, plants have succeeded in gaining a foothold, making it Europe's biggest vegetated shingle spit. The spit accommodates a healthy population of hares, Chinese water deer (escaped from deer parks), marsh harriers and barn owls.

You will soon have your first view of the castle a short distance inland.

After some time, you will come to a gate and a short section of boardwalk.

2 Cross, then turn right across the marsh to another riverbank – the Butley. Turn right to continue, with the marsh and castle on your right and the river on your left. Just after the river bends to the left, turn right down the waymarked path through a gate. Follow this track until you reach a tarmac lane.

There is evidence of Roman occupation of this area, and some of the finds can be seen in the museum within the castle.

3 Turn right onto the lane. Pass Richmond Farm cottages on the right, and after a further 100m (110yds), take the footpath on your left up a wide sandy track. Follow

this track as it bends to the right and then continues towards a wood. At the drive to Gedgrave Broom, bear right, remaining on the sandy track. Pass a couple of bungalows on your left and walk a little further to a third bungalow – Orford Lodge.

4 Turn right on a wide path towards the church. Follow this footpath to the village. Keep right onto Mundays Lane. Where this road bends left into the centre of the village, turn right past the Crown and Castle restaurant with rooms. Orford Castle is directly ahead.

On the stone font in Orford Church, there is the carving of a 'wild man'. It is reported that a man was once caught in the fishing nets here. He was covered in hair and did not speak. In response, the constable of the castle hung him upside down and tortured him, to no avail. Eventually, he escaped back to the sea.

ABOVE The village from the castle keep.
BELOW The castle and village as seen from between Points 2 and 3.

5 On leaving the castle, turn left on the tarmac road into the village centre. At the far end of the plaza, turn right and follow this road through the pretty village to return to the car park.

52 PENDENNIS CASTLE

Falmouth was important as the first landing point for ships arriving from the Mediterranean and across the Atlantic. Its deep estuary, known as Carrick Roads, also offered an excellent opportunity for enemy fleets to land.

Piracy and privateering were rife in the area, and in 1537 there was a battle between French and Spanish ships in Carrick Roads. A local man petitioned Henry VIII for fortifications, but his pleas were ignored. That is, until France and Spain formed a formal alliance the following year, thus increasing the risk of invasion. During the 1540s, Pendennis and St Mawes castles were built to protect Falmouth.

By the end of the century, England's relationship with Spain was even less amicable, so the fortifications at Pendennis were extended to include the geometric ramparts you circumnavigate on the 'Moat Walk'.

This created space for the parade ground and barracks inside the castle. The parade ground has previously housed a windmill and additional barracks as required.

The castle saw action during the British Civil Wars when it sheltered Royalists – until they had to surrender due to starvation. In WWII, the castle's guns were used again to protect the port.

WALK DETAILS

START/FINISH
Swanpool Beach car park, TR11 5BG

DISTANCE
10km (6¼ miles)

PARKING
At start, Falmouth Town railway station (join at Point 3)

PUBLIC TRANSPORT
Train to Falmouth Town (join walk at Point 3)

REFRESHMENTS
Pubs and cafés in Falmouth, café at Swanpool Beach and in castle (after entry gate)

TOILETS
Swanpool Beach, Gyllyngvase Beach, in castle (after entry gate)

BELOW Pendennis Castle's 15th century keep.

THE WALK

A coastal walk along the cliffs and beaches of Falmouth. The first loop gives views of the castle across the bay, and the second loop follows the coast path to and around Pendennis Point, then the castle moat, before returning along the coast path. This walk is mainly on tarmac.

1 Facing the sea, turn right on the road up the hill. After 200m (220yds), turn left onto the footpath signposted Coast Path. The sea is on your left and from here there is a good view of Pendennis Castle. After the first field on the right, turn right up a public footpath, straight uphill with the hedge on the right. When you reach the golf course, follow the footpath signs, taking care not to be hit by any flying balls. The path heads in a fairly straight line across the course. As you approach a short section of wall covered in plants, keep that to your right and the 16th tee to your left to find the next section of path ahead. After this, the route bears left downhill to join the Coast Path.

2 Turn left onto the coast path, and follow it back to Swanpool Beach, ignoring occasional paths off to the right that lead down to the sea. Continue on the Coast Path past the car park, in front of the line of beach huts, and along the cliffs to Gyllyngvase Beach.

3 Stay on the Coast Path for around 1.25km (¾ mile) after Gyllyngvase Beach, until you see the pedestrian access for Pendennis Castle on the left.

This section of the walk has great views of the castle.

4 Just before the drive to the castle, bear right down some steps onto a tarmac path below the level of the road, continuing in the same direction around the coast. After

PENDENNIS CASTLE

a while, this path rejoins the road. Continue with the sea on your right. When you reach the car park at the end of the peninsula, walk about halfway along and take the tarmac path down to the right to walk around Pendennis Point, including a visit to the small blockhouse guarding the Fal estuary.

> This blockhouse is a Tudor gun tower, possibly built at the same time as the castle. It is called Little Dennis, and would have been built to defend Crab Quay, which is a little further up the estuary and the best place to land on the peninsula. By 1600, it was part of a fort that enclosed the whole of Pendennis Point.

5 Stay on the path along the estuary beyond the car park. This path gradually drops. At a crossroads of paths, turn left uphill.

> The remains of Crab Quay are down and to the right.

Eventually, this path rises to meet the road. Turn right along the pavement until you reach a small path heading up through the woodland. This ends at the edge of the castle car park. If you miss the path, turn left to the car park and walk to the far end.

6 Turn left onto Moat Walk. This will take you around the perimeter of the castle to the entrance. Follow the path along the walls, down some steps, then along the track. Bear right to follow the track uphill, and then at the junction of paths, continue straight ahead with the gun battery on your left. At the next junction of paths, bear right up some steps back to the moat.

Past the castle entrance, take the drive downhill. At the end of the drive, retrace your steps to the car park and the end of the walk.

> Swanpool Lake is a Site of Special Scientific Interest (SSSI) that hosts a huge number of different birds, including tufted ducks, kingfishers and swans. This diverse bird life is fed by eels and other fish that enter the lake from the sea, and the myriad of insects that live in the reedbeds.

BELOW A section of coast path between Points 2 and 3.

TOP LEFT View across Carrick Roads from the blockhouse at Point 5.

LEFT View of the castle from between Points 2 and 3.

53 SCARBOROUGH CASTLE

Scarborough Castle has a striking silhouette, especially viewed from the south. The original Norman keep was badly damaged during a British Civil Wars siege, but the castle walls are in good condition on the south side.

During the Napoleonic Wars, there was a large barracks in the castle. It is thought that is why German warships targeted Scarborough and the castle early in WWI. In an attack that only lasted a few minutes, 500 shells landed on the castle and town, causing more damage to the castle and multiple deaths.

The castle is larger inside than it looks from the bay, as it splays from a narrow entrance. Much of this area is now covered in wildflower meadow, but during the 19th century it was used as a cricket pitch. In 1868, an Aboriginal Australian team played cricket here and demonstrated Aboriginal sporting skills. The local paper reported that 4,000 people attended one of their shows – and that during one performance, a spectator was killed when the part of the cliff he was standing on

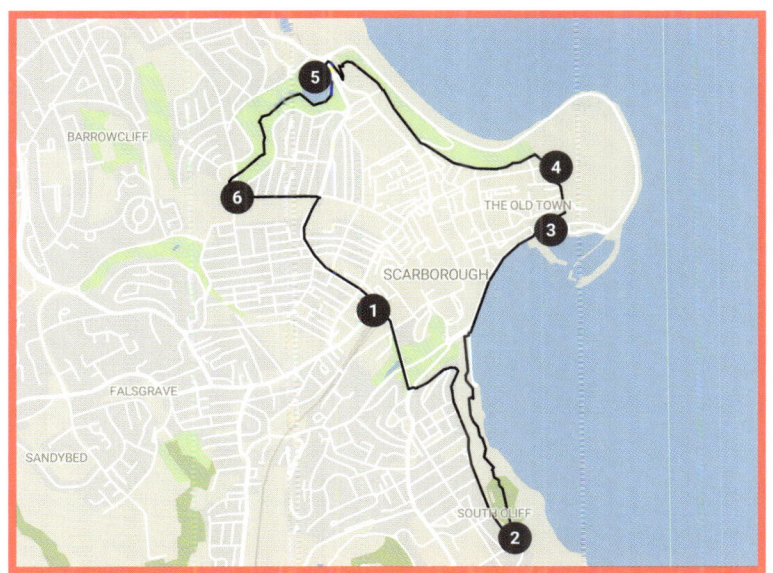

WALK DETAILS

START/FINISH
Scarborough railway station, YO11 1TN

DISTANCE
9km (5½ miles)

PARKING
Car parks in Scarborough near start

PUBLIC TRANSPORT
Train or coach to Scarborough

REFRESHMENTS
At start, along the seafront, at the castle (after entry gate), in Peasholm Park

TOILETS
At start, along the seafront, at the castle (after entry gate), in Peasholm Park

LEFT Scarborough Castle keep.

RIGHT Holbeck Clock Tower at Point 2.

collapsed due to coastal erosion. The building of Marine Drive in the early 20th century has reduced that particular threat.

The Walk
Clifftops and beaches both feature in this walk, giving fantastic views of Scarborough Castle and the Yorkshire

SCARBOROUGH CASTLE

coastline. There is also an Italianate garden, complete with statues and fountains, and a Japanese garden at the top of an island mountain! Some steep climbs and steps, mainly on tarmac or sand.

1 From the main entrance of the station, turn right then right again down Valley Bridge Road. After crossing the bridge, turn left along Belmont Road. This will lead you to South Cliff. Walk along the promenade with the sea on your left.

> *If you look south along the bay, you can see a break in the trees and a semicircular intrusion of land into the bay. This is the result of the landslide that destroyed the Holbeck Hall Hotel in 1993. The 60m-high (200ft) cliff is now 70m (230ft) further inland.*

Eventually, the path leads to Holbeck Clock Tower, just this side of the landslide site.

TOP RIGHT The keep as seen from between Points 4 and 5.

BELOW RIGHT The castle from the south, as seen between Points 2 and 3.

BELOW The Japanese Garden in Peasholm Park between Points 5 and 6.

2 From here, you can either work your way back through the gardens that adorn the cliffs (including the Italianate garden mentioned in the walk summary), slowly reaching the seashore, or continue on the tarmac path ahead for a more direct route down and the opportunity to walk back along the sand. The route takes you all the way along the front to the harbour.

3 Opposite the harbour, turn up the side of the Newcastle Packet. At the top of the steep slope, turn right onto East Sandgate. After a short distance, follow the road around to the left and uphill. This is Castlegate. Just before the road reaches Paradise, turn right up some steps under trees. When you reach a tarmac path, continue ahead up more steps, which lead to the castle entrance.

> *Turn left for a short detour to St Mary's church, where Anne Brontë is buried. This church used to be much bigger, but was largely destroyed during the British Civil Wars. Parliamentarians fired on the castle from the church, so the castle cannons were fired back, causing significant damage to both buildings.*

SCARBOROUGH CASTLE

4 With your back to the castle gatehouse, take the path on the right that rises gradually and soon provides views over North Bay and the white pyramids of the Sealife Centre. This path leads to the promenade. Follow this along the top of the bay, and when Queens Parade bends to the left, continue ahead, remaining at the top of the cliffs. At the end of the terrace, follow this path around to the left. Fork left, maintaining your elevation, then right at the next junction of paths onto a path that winds its way gently downhill, ending at Columbus Ravine.

5 Turn right towards the roundabout, then turn left before you reach it and enter Peasholm Park. Turn left, then right over the footbridge. Turn left around the island, past the cascade. On the far side of the island, take the steps up to the Japanese garden at the top of the hill. Return to the lakeside and complete your circumnavigation of the island.

During the summer, the lake in Peasholm Park is home to Naval Warfare, a battle using model ships, replete with sound effects, smoke and aeroplanes.

Cross the footbridge and turn right around the lake. When you reach the ponds that feed the lake, turn left and follow the path uphill alongside the ponds and then the stream. At the confluence of streams, fork left. At the next fork, with the stream on your left, bear right, rising above the stream. Fork left just before passing beneath the road bridge. Turn left onto a path that leads to a small roundabout.

6 Cross to Dean Road and keep the cemetery to your right as you head downhill. At the end of the cemetery, turn right and follow the A165 back to the station.

SCARBOROUGH CASTLE 227

54 ST MICHAEL'S MOUNT

Until around 2000 BC, Mount's Bay was wet woodland. When the bay was inundated by the sea, St Michael's Mount became a tidal island and is likely to have also become a centre for trade.

Legend has it that, in AD 495, fishermen were warned off the rocks by St Michael, and since then, the site has been a destination for pilgrims. The Normans established a priory here in 1135, subservient to Mont-St-Michel. That arrangement continued until 1414, when control was relinquished because of the Hundred Years' War with France.

The mount survived a six-month siege in 1473 during the Wars of the Roses. In 1549, the next siege was more successful. The local gentry were taken as hostages as part of the rebellion against church services being held in English – most locals only spoke Cornish. The mount was also refortified during the British Civil Wars in favour of the Royalists.

There has been a garden on the mount for around 250 years. Like the buildings, it was extended in Victorian times. The south-facing rocks absorb heat during the day and release it at night, creating a climate that suits many exotic plants, especially succulents.

THE WALK

Follow the ancient pilgrimage route of St Michael's Way around a wetland nature reserve to Ludgvan, Tremenheere Sculpture Gardens and Gulval to return to Marazion along the shore. Fantastic views of St Michael's Mount. The nature reserve path can flood during high tides. There are several stiles on this route.

WALK DETAILS

START/FINISH
St Michael's Mount car park, TR17 0EG

DISTANCE
10.5km (6½ miles)

PARKING
At start, Long Rock car park TR20 8HZ (cheaper) and Marazion car park, both between Point 5 and finish

PUBLIC TRANSPORT
Bus from Penzance to The Kite Loft (Marazion)

REFRESHMENTS
Pubs and cafés in Marazion, tea shops at Tremenheere Sculpture Gardens and Gulval

TOILETS
In Marazion and at Marazion car park

1 From the entrance to the car park, turn left. Follow the busy road for approximately 50m (55yds), then take the right fork past the entrance to the overflow car park. Turn left at the road junction just after the caravan park, then take the footpath on the right at the far end of the narrow bridge. After a while, follow the path right over a footbridge.

RIGHT St Michael's Mount as seen from between Points 6 and 7.

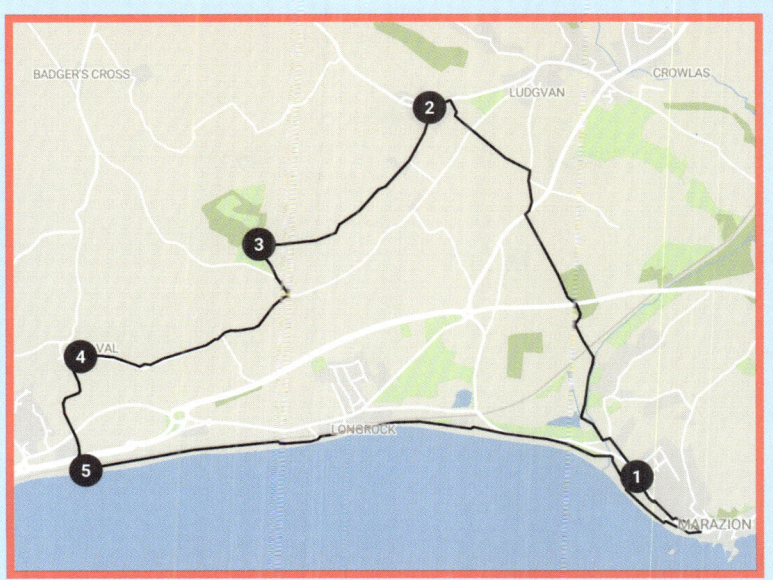

You are now on St Michael's Way, an ancient pilgrimage route for Welsh and Irish pilgrims heading to Santiago de Compostela in northern Spain. They would arrive in Cornwall by boat on the north coast, and then walk over to Marazion for their onward journey from the harbour on St Michael's Mount, avoiding the treacherous seas around the tip of Cornwall. Goods would take a similar route over land.

ABOVE Part of the path between Points 1 and 2.

ABOVE Part of the route between Points 1 and 2.

Cross the railway line, then take the boardwalk over the marsh and then through a wet woodland. When you reach the A-road, cross it and take the footpath ahead and slightly to the left.

The path now follows the edge of fields until you reach another A-road. You're aiming for the church tower visible on the skyline ahead. At the road, cross and head up the quiet lane almost opposite, signposted Ludgvan Leaze. After about 100m (110yds), cross the stone stile on your left, and follow the path along the edge of fields up to the village of Ludgvan. Turn left past the church.

2 Turn left down Eglos Road.

After a short distance, look to the left for views over St Michael's Mount.

Where this lane bends to the left, continue ahead down a stone track. Where this track bends to the right, continue ahead through a five-bar gate. Penzance can now be seen directly ahead.

After a few metres, the track dissipates. Take the narrow path heading downhill directly ahead. Continue on this path, following the stylised scallop shell waymarkers as it crosses quiet lanes and fields and joins a track. At the end of the track, continue ahead on a footpath along the left side of the field, which emerges near Tremenheere Sculpture Gardens and tearoom. Both are worth a visit if you have time.

3 To continue on the route, turn left down the track past the tearoom.
When you reach the road, continue in the same direction. At the end of the road, turn right onto a quiet country lane. Shortly after the first road on the left, look for a stylised shell waymarker leading you to the right and then along the edge of the field running parallel to the road. Eventually, the path joins the road. Continue ahead into the village.

4 At the triangular road junction by the church, stay left. The church is on your right. Take the first road on the left, heading gently downhill towards the sea. After some time, head straight over the crossroads, over another road and under the railway to reach the bay.

5 Turn left on the coast path to return to Marazion. Head through the long-stay car park to the shore, then turn left, with St Michael's Mount on your right. Continue in the same direction until you reach The Square (which is triangular). Turn left onto North Street in front of the Marazion Hotel. After a while, you pass the old town well and then meet a through road.

The town well was used until 1870, when mains water was brought to the town.

At the road, turn right, back to the long-stay car park.

LEFT St Michael's Mount as seen from the final stretch of the walk.

55 STIRLING CASTLE

WALK DETAILS

START/FINISH
Stirling railway station, FK8 1FP

DISTANCE
7.75km (4¾ miles)

PARKING
Car parks in Stirling, Park and Ride

PUBLIC TRANSPORT
Train to Stirling

REFRESHMENTS
Pubs and cafés near start, café in castle (after entry gate)

TOILETS
In castle (after entry gate)

The renovation and restoration of Stirling Castle is breathtaking, providing the finest complex of late-medieval and Renaissance buildings in Scotland.

The lava from a volcanic eruption provides the basalt base, some 76m (250ft) high, upon which the original fortifications were added about 3,000 years ago. Stirling was at the crossroads of routes north to south and west to east, and commanded the most convenient crossing of the River Forth.

Early tribes, Romans, Britons, Picts, Angles and Norsemen battled for domination of the crag, and Stirling Castle was often besieged. During the Wars of Scottish Independence around the turn of the 14th century, it changed hands no fewer than eight times.

Early in the 16th century, the Treaty of Perpetual Peace between England and Scotland meant that the castle no longer needed to be fortified. James IV started to build a castle designed to impress rather than defend and painted it gold to demonstrate his wealth. His son, James V, built a palace full of symbolism to present himself as a king equal to any

RIGHT The Beheading Stone at Point 5.

BELOW Stirling Castle with its golden Great Hall as seen from the cemetery between Points 5 and 6.

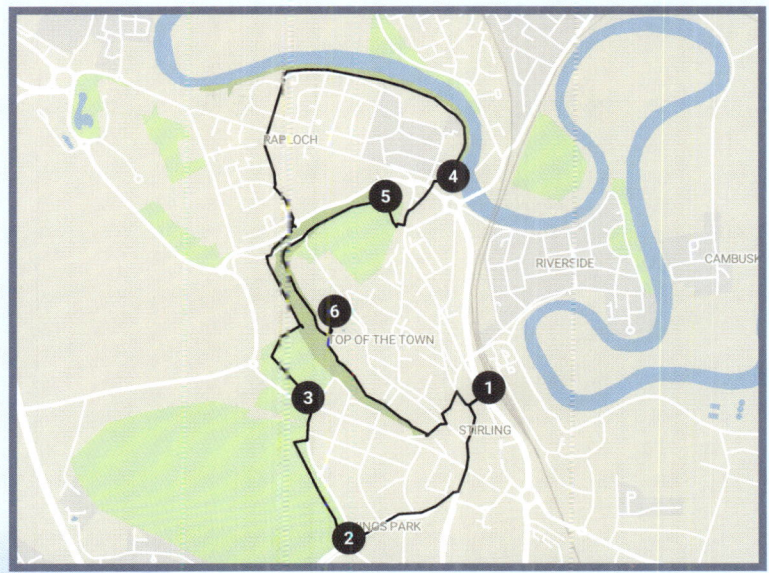

in Europe. This is the period to which the castle has been restored, using master craftspeople to recreate paintings, carvings and tapestries.

The Walk
The bustling city centre contrasts with a fine park, then the geometric ridges of the King's and Queen's Knots historic gardens below the clifftop castle. Walk along the River Forth to the 1400s bridge. Keep your head as you climb to the Beheading Stone and up to the castle.

1 Walk directly away from the main station entrance, uphill. At the T-junction by the Stirling Arcade, turn left. Follow the road to the right (Murray Place and then Port Street). Head straight over the traffic lights, then fork right at the clock towards Kings Park. At the mini roundabout, continue ahead to the entrance.

STIRLING CASTLE

2 Head into the park. Pass the fountain and then turn right. At a junction of paths, continue ahead. At the next junction, just before the golf clubhouse, turn right towards the road, and then left along the road. Where the road bends to the left, cross and enter the field through the ornate gates.

3 Take the path directly towards and over the King's and Queen's Knots, historically part of the castle's formal gardens. At the far end of the Knots, turn right towards the castle (clearly visible on the skyline). Head through the small gap in the corner of the wall and gently uphill. After a short flight of steps, turn left through a gap in the wall along the side of the hill. At a T-junction with a minor road, turn right and then almost immediately left onto another path downhill. This path drops down to a roundabout. Turn left onto Glendevon Drive, then right to stay on Glendevon Drive. At the end of the drive, continue ahead across the plaza then cross Drip Road to take Woodside Road. Follow this road around to the right.

The river is now on your left, although not often visible. After a while, a fantastic view of the castle opens up to your right, including onto the golden Great Hall, which has been painted in what is thought to be its original colour.

Continue along to the stone bridge on the left.

This is the Stirling Bridge, the site of a decisive victory by William Wallace over the Anglo-Normans.

TOP LEFT Stirling Bridge at Point 4.

LEFT The King's Knot at Point 3.

4 At the base of the bridge, turn right. Turn left under the subway, then right up Gowan Hill after the large stone building. Turn right between the huge stone gateposts, then right again signposted Mote Hill. At the next junction of paths, turn right to the top of the old hill fort to see the Beheading Stone and fantastic views over the Forth Valley, Wallace Monument and Ochil Hills.

5 Retrace your steps to the junction of paths, then turn right downhill. At a crossroads of paths, continue ahead. At the next junction, turn right with Gowan Hill on your left.

(When you reach the road, take a 200m (220yd) detour to the left and into the cemetery for an incredible view of the castle.)

Head back down the road and continue along the path around the hill, which is now above the road. The castle is high up on your left. This path ends at the cemetery. Turn left up the hill to enter the castle.

6 After visiting the castle take the steps on the right back down to the graveyard. At the first junction of paths, continue ahead with the graveyard on your left and the valley on your right.

Take a short detour to the left to visit the Church of the Holy Rude where James V was crowned, and the 16th-century hospital. Return to the path.

After the hospital, you can see the old town walls on your left. On reaching a road, turn left past the public library. Skirt around the right-hand edge of the clock tower (Athenaeum), along Baker Street. Turn right down Friars Street. At the end, turn right and then left to return to the station.

THREAVE CASTLE

Threave Castle is considered one of the best examples of the Scottish tower houses built after the conclusion of the Wars of Independence with England in the 14th century. These wars were started after the Anglo-Normans finally conquered Wales, and Edward I had built (although not quite finished) the Ring of Iron castles in North Wales in order to quell any further rebellion there.

The tower is surrounded on three sides by later artillery fortifications, the oldest in Scotland and used in the siege of Threave. The siege was won by King James II. It resulted in the downfall of the Douglases, a powerful noble family until that point. In 1640, the castle was partially demolished and abandoned after it was surrendered by Royalists to end the Covenanting Army's siege.

Archaeological excavations suggest that there were important buildings alongside the tower house, blowing the theory that these great towers stood on their own. These buildings were demolished when the artillery fortifications were built, so they are not visible today.

Now, the tower house stands as a romantic ruin, reached only by a ferry across the River Dee or by using the hidden underwater causeway – if you know where to find it!

WALK DETAILS

START/FINISH
Carlingwark Loch, Castle Douglas

DISTANCE
10.75km (6⅔ miles)

PARKING
On road near start, car parks in Castle Douglas or at Threave Nature Reserve DG7 1TJ (Point 4)

PUBLIC TRANSPORT
Bus from Dumfries to Whitepark Road (Castle Douglas)

REFRESHMENTS
Refreshments: Pubs and cafés in Castle Douglas

TOILETS
At start and Point 4

BELOW Threave Castle from across the River Dee.

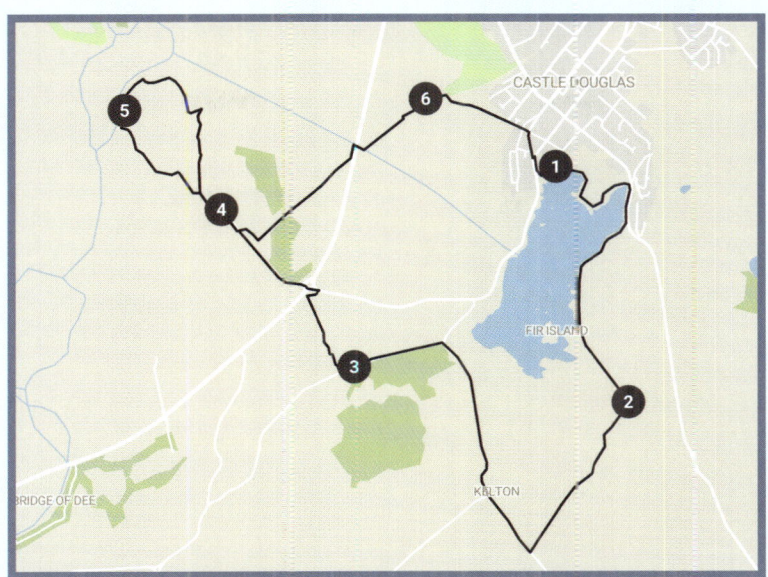

THE WALK

A mostly flat walk through interesting wetland habitats. First, a loch, then a marsh, then Threave Nature Reserve, all leading to the reflection of Threave Castle in the River Dee. From March to August, there's also the opportunity to see ospreys nesting near the river and peregrines nesting in the castle.

1 Make your way down to the loch side and turn left along the bank. The path continues down the side and beyond the end of the loch, and eventually reaches a T-junction of paths.

2 Turn right towards Mid Kelton on a boardwalk across the marshes at the southern end of the loch. When you reach a small lane, turn right and follow it until you reach the entrance to Threave Garden.

Threave Garden is owned by the National Trust for Scotland, and is home to the School of Heritage Gardening. The

3 Shortly afterwards, take the path between two houses. Take the gate on the left to meander through the woods. At the end of this path, cross the track ahead and continue in a similar direction through the gate opposite. Continue along this path and through another pair of gates to a couple of houses and then right and left to a roundabout. Take the second exit to Threave Castle. On entering Threave Nature Reserve, take the footpath along the left side of the lane to the car park and farm.

ABOVE One of the paths across Threave Nature Reserve.

The nature reserve has a 100-year plan to re-naturalise the land after intensive farming damaged the ecosystem. They have allowed the Dee to breach the raised bank, creating an extensive wetland area, and cows graze the land in a controlled fashion to help it recover.

garden has been designed by students and showcases many different styles.

Turn left at the next junction. After about 700m (½ mile), you pass another entrance to Threave Garden.

4 Turn left then right between the buildings towards the castle. As you reach the end of the wall, the castle is now in view ahead. Turn left and then follow the path to the right towards the castle. At the next junction of paths, the castle is just the other side of the River Dee. Turn right towards the castle ferry.

5 Continue along the path to the bird hide.

This is where you may be able to see osprey and peregrine falcons on their nests, as well as otters sliding through the water. The osprey migrate between here and Senegal. The same couple arrives back here each spring within a few days of each other and around the same date each year – 20 March. They soon mate and build their nest on the platform provided by the National Trust for Scotland. The nest is about 1.8m (6ft) in diameter although it looks tiny, even through the scopes set up for visitors. Once the chicks are big enough, a ringer climbs the tree that houses the platform and rings them, so that they can be tracked. It seems that the adult birds are familiar with this procedure, and luckily for the ringers, watch on calmly instead of trying to protect their young.

From the hide, continue along the path away from the river, and then into woodland. At the junction, turn right towards Kelton Mains. This path takes you back to the junction at the end of the wall. Turn left back towards the farm.

ABOVE A boardwalk across Threave Nature Reserve.

BELOW Carlingwark Loch as seen from the first section of the walk.

Once through the buildings, head back down the path to the side of the drive. When it turns to meet the drive, cross onto the path on the far side and follow it as it curves around to meet the old railway line. Turn left. After some distance, this path leads under the A-road and eventually ends at a farm track.

6 Turn right. When you reach a T-junction, turn right towards some trees. After a couple of hundred metres, turn left into the park to return to the start.

TINTAGEL CASTLE

Tintagel Castle is one of the world's most romantic and mystical. Perched on a windswept headland that is rapidly becoming an island, it is the legendary setting for King Arthur's conception and birth. Merlin's Cave runs underneath the island and, in the right light, it emanates a magical golden glow.

Archaeologists have found evidence of Romans here in the 3rd and 4th centuries. In the dark ages that followed, it was probably a seat of the kings of Dumnonia, as the occupants of the headland ate olives and drank wine from the Mediterranean – foodstuffs that were not readily available.

In the 12th century, the first legendary link was made between Tintagel and King Arthur, which may be why Richard, Earl of Cornwall, chose Tintagel for his new castle. The castle was finished around 1230, but Richard would not have spent much time here. He joined the Crusades in 1240 and ruled Germany from 1257 until his death 15 years later.

After that, the castle mainly deteriorated until it came into the care of English Heritage. In the 19th and 20th centuries, the area became a hive of industry, with slate and galena (silver-lead ore) mines giving rise to the stone platforms clinging on to the nearby cliffs.

WALK DETAILS

START/FINISH
The Wootons Inn, Tintagel PL34 0DD

DISTANCE
7.25km (4½ miles)

PARKING
Car parks in Tintagel and Trebarwith Strand PL34 0HB (join walk at Point 5)

PUBLIC TRANSPORT
Bus from Bodmin to Tintagel visitor centre (change at Valley Truckle)

REFRESHMENTS
Pubs and cafés in Tintagel, pub at Trebarwith Strand

TOILETS
In Tintagel near Visitor Centre

LEFT The mainland part of the castle as seen from the island.

The Walk
The walk heads south along the rugged Cornish cliffs to Trebarwith Strand, a small village with a superb beach when the tide is out and a popular pub with a large terrace overlooking the sea. The return leg follows quiet lanes inland via the Norman church of St Materiana.

1 From the pub, walk down Castle Lane towards the castle. Just before the ticket booth, take the path left over the stream and diagonally up the side of the valley, heading towards the footbridge over the eroded gap between the two parts of the castle.

2 At the top, continue on the South West Coast Path along the clifftops with the sea to your right to the tiny Tintagel Youth Hostel.

As you pass the Tintagel Youth Hostel – and in other places along this stretch of coast – you can see the stone platforms that were used to winch slates and ore down to ships below. Some of the slate and ore quarries are also visible.

TINTAGEL CASTLE

ABOVE King Arthur in the castle.

3 Continue south along the coast path.

> On 17 October 1886, the Sarah Anderson was shipwrecked off the coast here, leading to the loss of 15 lives. An inquiry concluded that the ship was sound on leaving port, and that the wreck was caused by stormy weather, rather than the owner's negligence. A few days after the ship was seen to sink, the captain's masonic certificate, a nightshirt bearing his wife's name and the ship's flag were washed onto the shore, confirming the name of the ship. While the ship was in distress, the coastguard was called, but it was too stormy to launch the rescue boat.

4 Drop steeply down to Trebarwith Strand for refreshments or a visit to the beach.

5 When you are ready to return, retrace your steps back up to the clifftops. Take the first path on the right towards a couple of houses. This path follows the line of a Cornish hedge and then passes between two of them before reaching the buildings.

> Cornish hedges are planted along the top of a drystone wall filled with earth. The herringbone style of construction you see here is distinctive. Over time, these walls support a wide range of wildlife, as plants grow in the soil and animals shelter in the gaps between stones. It is estimated that there are over 20,000 miles of Cornish hedges.

Follow the drive that leads away from the houses skirting the village of Treknow and onto the B-road.

6 Turn left onto the B-road for a short distance. When the road bends sharply right, continue straight ahead on a minor road to a wooden-clad bungalow called Trevillick Farm.

7 Just beyond the bungalow, ignore the path to the left and take the left fork towards the church that is now visible on the horizon. At another fork by a National Trust sign, stay right and follow the track to the church.

> St Materiana's is about two hundred years older than the castle and worth a visit if you are interested in Norman churches. Look out for the stained-glass window dedicated to John Douglas Cook, founder of the Saturday Review, the lifebuoy from a shipwreck at nearby Bossiney Cove in 1893 and the stone in the south transept that is inscribed with the name of Roman emperor Licinius.

8 Follow the path out through the churchyard and back into the village. When you reach the main road, the Wootons Inn is on your left.

TOP The island part of the castle from the mainland (credit: iStock).

ABOVE Merlin's Cave.

58 TOWER OF LONDON

WALK DETAILS

START/FINISH
Tower Hill Tube station

DISTANCE
7.5km (4²⁄₃ miles)

PARKING
Several car parks in the area

PUBLIC TRANSPORT
Tower Hill Tube, St Paul's or Monument Tube (join walk at Point 4), London Bridge railway station (joint walk at Point 2)

REFRESHMENTS
Plentiful options along the route

TOILETS
At start, near HMS *Belfast* between Points 1 & 2, Borough Market near the *Golden Hinde* between Points 2 & 3

Imagine living in the low-rise London of the 11th century. William has just conquered England but is fearful of revolt, so he has built a series of castles. Arguably the most important is the Tower of London. The enormous stone keep is unlike anything you have ever seen and dominates the landscape for miles. William is a powerful man, and this castle is designed to ensure that everyone knows it.

Fast forward almost 200 years, and Henry III and Edward I (the latter a great castle-builder in Wales) both expanded it until it was the biggest concentric castle in England. Henry III painted the tower white, at which point it became known as the 'White Tower'.

It is probably best known for housing the crown jewels, so it is still actively used

BELOW The Tower of London as seen from the south of the River Thames between Points 1 & 2.

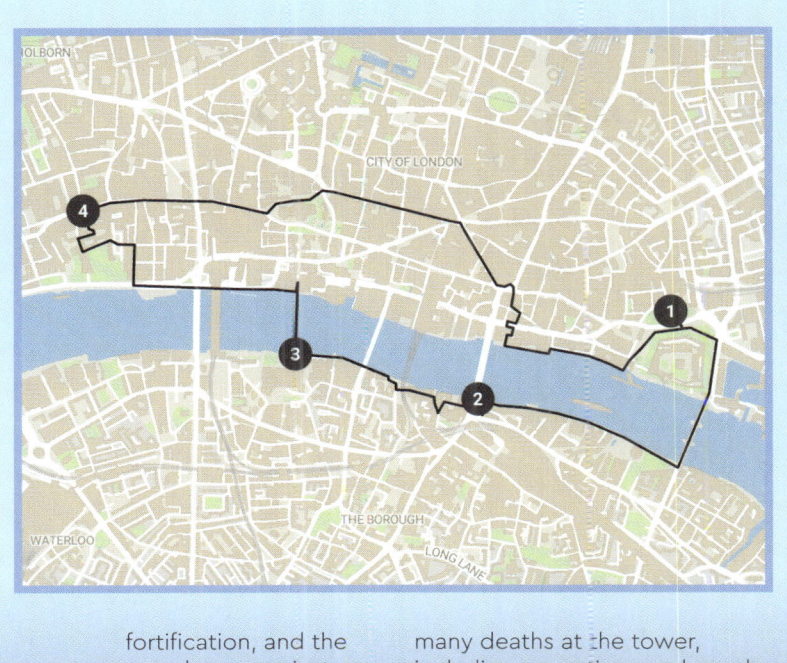

fortification, and the guards are not just for show. For much of its life, it was also a prison, where anyone deemed a threat to national security was held, sometimes in luxurious conditions, sometimes terrible. There have been many deaths at the tower, including executions and murders, and it is, unsurprisingly, reputed to be haunted.

THE WALK

An exciting walk around some of London's iconic places, including Tower Bridge, London Bridge, Southwark Cathedral, the *Golden Hinde*, Shakespeare's Globe Theatre,

the Inns of Court, St Paul's Cathedral and Monument. Easy walking on flat tarmac, except for a few steps. Fantastic views of many iconic sights, including of the Tower of London.

1 **From Tower Hill station, cross the road in front of the Tower of London using the underpass by the giant sundial.** This takes you to the moat, which is now a wildflower meadow. Turn left and walk around the tower until you reach Tower Bridge. Cross the bridge and take the steps down on the far side, to the embankment. Turn right and follow Queen's Walk, with the river on your right.

> *From here, there are great views of the Tower of London.*

The next bridge you reach is London Bridge.

2 **From here, the route continues upstream, but it does not run along the riverbank. Climb up the steps to London Bridge, and then turn left.** Bear left up a ramp with The Shard directly ahead, then take the stairs down on the left. Continue to the bottom of the steps, then take the underpass. After a few metres, you pass Southwark Cathedral on your left.

> *The cathedral has several impressive stained-glass windows and a memorial to their parishioner William Shakespeare.*

ABOVE The ancient Tower of London holds its own against the modern city.

After the cathedral, follow the road around to the left, then take the next road on the right, Cathedral Street. About halfway down the dry dock that holds the Golden Hinde, turn left onto Pickfords Wharf.

> *The ruins ahead are the remains of the palace of the bishops of Winchester. It was once on the banks of the river, which indicates how much the course of the river has changed.*

Pass under a railway arch, then turn right to the river and left along it. Pass beneath Southwark Bridge, and continue along the river past Shakespeare's Globe Theatre to the Millennium Bridge. The Tate Modern art gallery is on the left.

3 **Cross the river here. St Paul's Cathedral is directly ahead of you.**

> *When it was first built, the Millennium Bridge was also known as the 'Wobbly Bridge', as it swung wildly before dampeners were added to make it more stable.*

On the far side of the bridge, take a sharp left down some steps to the riverbank. Turn right along the embankment. After another two bridges, look for Temple Avenue on

 TOWER OF LONDON

your right and turn up it. Take the first left, Tudor Street. Head under the arch into the Inner Temple. Continue ahead with Paper Buildings on your left and a red brick building on your right. Pass the Inner Temple Garden on your left, which is open from 12:30pm on weekdays. Pass underneath another arch and turn right. When you reach Brick Court, turn right towards Temple Church. Turn left around the near end of the church, and then to Fleet Street.

4 Turn right and follow Fleet Street until you reach St Paul's Cathedral.
Walk to the far end of the cathedral, with the building on your right. Cross the road at the end, and follow Cheapside until you reach Bank, a busy junction surrounded by historic buildings.

Fork right down Lombard Street, then stay ahead on King William Street. At the next multi-road junction, turn left and then right down Fish Street Hill to reach Monument, which commemorates the Great Fire of London in 1666.

Turn left along the plaza, then right downhill onto Pudding Lane. At the bottom of Pudding Lane, turn right onto Lower Thames Street, then left to cross it, left back the way you came, and right down to the riverside path. At the river, turn left and follow the embankment until you reach the Tower of London. Turn left and walk around the moat to return to Tower Hill Station.

ABOVE Monument, as seen on the final leg of the walk.

BELOW Tower Bridge, crossed at the start of the walk.

59 URQUHART CASTLE

Once one of Scotland's largest castles, what we see of Urquhart Castle today dates from the 13th to 16th centuries. During its 500 years in service, Urquhart saw a great deal of conflict. During the Wars of Independence, the castle passed from one side to the other. The conflict continued, with frequent raids on the castle by the Lords of the Isles. It seems that the site was of too great a strategic importance to allow it to fall into enemy hands. It was also too expensive to maintain against a continuous series of raids, so in 1692 the English government decided that enough was enough. The troops departed and blew the castle up behind them.

Urquhart's ruins remain, offering glimpses into medieval lives. The water gate reminds us that most transportation during this period was by water. However, the landward side of the castle was also well defended – by an unusually wide and deep ditch crossed by a drawbridge.

This strategic site on the shores of Loch Ness was used well before the castle was built. An Iron Age fort stood here, and it is thought that a Pictish nobleman had a residence here in the 6th century.

WALK DETAILS

START/FINISH
Junction of the A82 and Great Glen Way at Lewiston. Nearest postcode IV63 6UN

DISTANCE
9.25km (5¾ miles)

PARKING
On road at or near start

PUBLIC TRANSPORT
Coach from Inverness to Urquhart Castle car park

REFRESHMENTS
Cafés in castle (after entry gate), Lewiston and Drumnadrochit

TOILETS
In castle (after entry gate), Drumnadrochit car park

THE WALK

A gentle valley stroll, then up through woodland. Rewilded woodlands provide beauty and peace. The route descends towards Loch Ness with a viewpoint over the castle. A short stretch alongside the road leads to the castle and then back towards Lewiston. A meadow and woodland walk finish off the route.

1 From the picnic tables, take the lane away from the main road.

This is part of the Great Glen Way, marked with blue waymarkers. The route follows this Great Trail for some distance uphill. Where the lane bends to the left, take the drive ahead towards the Clunebeg Estate, along the bottom of the valley. Where the drive forks, keep right. Eventually, you will pass Clunebeg Lodge on your left. Continue ahead on the footpath. Follow the path uphill and around to the left into forestry, following the blue waymarkers. At the end of the path, turn left onto the stony track uphill. When you reach the tarmac lane, turn right, again following signs for the Great Glen Way, to the first drive on the left.

LEFT Urquhart Castle stands on the shores of Loch Ness (credit: iStock).

BELOW The route through the woods between Points 2 and 3.

2 This is where the route leaves the Great Glen Way. Turn up the drive towards Drovers Lodge. After about 200m (220yds), close to the crest of the track, turn left onto a footpath with a fence on your right.

> *Bilberries cover the ground here under the trees. Further along the path where the trees are less dense, heather dominates. The trees are covered with mosses and lichens.*

Keep the fence on your right until you reach a wide gate, with some deer fencing on the left. At this point, continue ahead with the deer fence a few metres to your left. Continue to the corner of the deer fencing, where there is a pedestrian gate into the fenced area and a junction of paths. Ignore the pedestrian gate and continue ahead along an old track. After another 50m (55yds) or so, ignore the track heading downhill on the left and continue ahead more gently downhill. After a short distance, there is an old shed in the woods on the right. Shortly after this, fork left. This track gently descends around the hill on the right. Eventually, you will reach a house on the left.

3 Join their drive and continue downhill onto a tarmac lane. Just before a sharp turn to the left and Strone Castle Cottage on the right, take the narrow path opposite the gate behind and above the cottage. After a short distance, there are fantastic views down to the castle on the lochside below.

Return to the tarmac lane and continue downhill to the A-road. Turn right along the pavement at the side of the road for a closer view of the castle and to visit it.

URQUHART CASTLE

4 Return along the A-road past the tarmac lane and continue until the pavement drops slightly away from the road. At the end of the crash barrier, take the path on the right through a field gate and diagonally down the meadow towards the loch. At the field gate at the bottom of the hill, turn left to continue on the route or take a short detour down to the side of the loch.

At the next farm gate, continue ahead. At the end of this stretch, there is another field gate on the left. Ignore this and head right into the woods. This path bends to the left and follows the line of the river for a while. At the next junction of paths, turn left across the end of a yard to the A-road. Turn right along the path next to the road or drop down to the grassy track running parallel to it. If you choose the grassy track, join the pavement at the side of the road at the next yard (opposite a campsite). Continue along the road to finish the walk.

BELOW Part of the path between Points 2 and 3.

BOTTOM The castle as seen from Point 4.

URQUHART CASTLE

WINDSOR CASTLE

Windsor Castle is unique in the UK because it remains the home of the monarch and is still used for affairs of state. Immediately after the Norman Conquest, the victors built a castle in London called the White Tower (now known as the Tower of London, Walk 58). A ring of other castles was built around London, all a day's march from the White Tower and a day's march from each other. Windsor is one of those castles, and the only one to remain in good condition.

Unlike the White Tower and many other Norman castles, Windsor was never rendered and limewashed. Perhaps the Normans thought that the light buff stone stood out well enough, and indeed the castle is prominent in the landscape, even though it's only on a slight rise.

In 1992, a fire destroyed 115 rooms of the castle. Elizabeth II, the reigning monarch, took the opportunity to rebuild with the help of master craftspeople. The result is impressive. St George's Hall's replacement roof is a work of great skill and beauty.

WALK DETAILS

START/FINISH
Windsor & Eton Central railway station, SL4 1PJ

DISTANCE
11.75km (7⅓ miles)

PARKING
Windsor Great Park car parks (join between Points 4 & 5)

PUBLIC TRANSPORT
Train to Windsor & Eton Central railway station or Windsor & Eton Riverside railway station

REFRESHMENTS
Pubs and cafés in Windsor

TOILETS
At start

BELOW Approaching Windsor Castle from the Long Walk (credit: Mistervlad/Shutterstock).

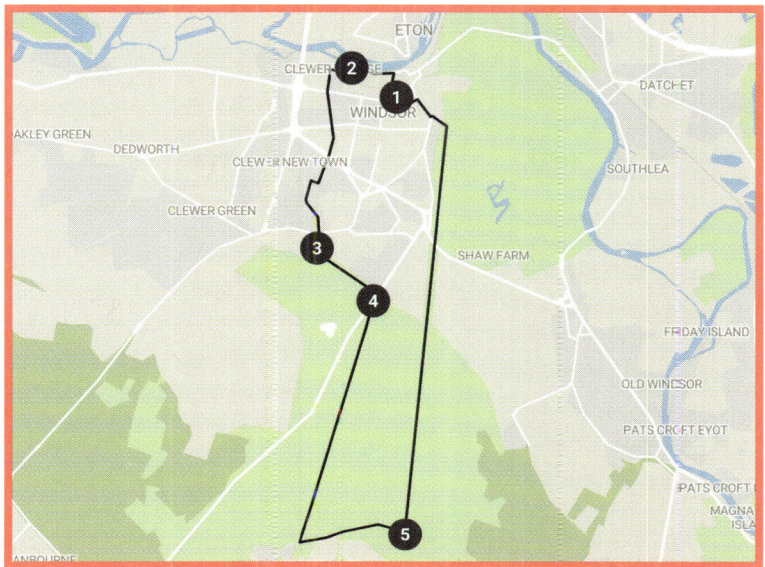

Prince Philip led the renovation of the Lantern Lobby, which now rises like a 1920s Elven hall. It is stunning.

THE WALK

This walk starts with a stroll along the River Thames before crossing the town to Windsor Great Park. The route rises to the ridge overlooking Windsor, then drops back along The Long Walk – an avenue of trees that leads directly to the castle. Easy walking with fabulous views.

1 With your back to the ticket office, walk past the front of the steam train and the metal bull sculpture to exit the station. Drop down the steps, and turn right at the bottom, then right again at the far end of the ramp down some more steps. Turn left at the bottom, then right under the railway. Continue ahead past the brick maze and Jubilee Fountain to the river. Turn left along the river and continue until you reach the Hawker Hurricane aeroplane.

2 Turn left then right under the arches and in front of the houses on Barry Avenue. Take the first left onto Vansittart Road. Continue ahead over several road junctions then down a leafy lane between parks and under the main road. Where this lane meets a road, turn left. This is York Avenue. At the end, turn right then take the first left onto Bulkeley Avenue. Eventually, you will reach the B3022. Turn right then take the first left down St Leonard's Road. Turn left through the football ground car park to the gate at the far end.

On your right is Windsor Great Park, an old royal hunting ground that is part of the Crown Estate, now open to the public.

3 Through the gate, continue ahead for about 750m (½ mile) until you reach a road.

4 At the road, look diagonally right for the statue on the ridge. This is the furthest point of the walk. To reach it, look further to the right for an avenue of trees. Turn right, cross the road and walk up this avenue. This is Queen Anne's Ride. Follow it almost to the millstone monument you can see on the skyline.

> As you walk up the Ride, look back for good views of the castle keep.

Just before reaching the millstone monument, a tarmac drive crosses the grassy ride. Turn left here. After a while, this drive leads through some tall gates into the deer park. After the gates, fork right up into the trees. Where this track bends steeply to the right, take the grassy footpath straight ahead.

When this path exits the woods, you will see the enormous statue of King George III directly ahead.

> If you look to the left, you will also see the central London skyline.
> As you approach the statue, look left down the avenue of trees to the castle. This is The Long Walk and is the route back down into Windsor. After the British Civil Wars, the monarchy was abolished, and Britain was a republic for 11 years. At that point, the monarchy was restored. The new king, Charles II, was highly influenced by French architecture and introduced several avenues into the park, including The Long Walk. The Long Walk is unusual, as it is an avenue with two lines of trees each side of the ride. The nearest are horse chestnuts, with a row of plane trees behind.
> As you descend, look behind you for great views of the statue. The views of the castle ahead are magnificent.

5 Follow the avenue down, through the park gates and over the A-road to the castle gates. Turn left into the town. At the T-junction, turn right. Pass the Guildhall, which houses Windsor and Royal Borough Museum, and take the next road on the left, opposite the statue of Queen Victoria. After the big clock on the right, take the first right – Goswell Hill – which returns you to the railway station.

TOP RIGHT The River Thames between Points 1 and 2.

RIGHT The Hawker Hurricane at Point 2.

BELOW The Long Walk leading to Windsor Castle from Point 5 (credit: Bildagentur Zoonar GmbH/Shutterstock).

ACKNOWLEDGEMENTS

First and foremost, I would like to thank my husband Mike, who taught me to love castles. He also helped me with the research for this book and acted as chauffeur during my research tour. I would also like to thank all the castle tour guides who were so informative and patient with our questioning; those castle owners who allowed me free entry; Cadw, English Heritage, Historic Environment Scotland and all others that have taken responsibility for protecting such an important part of our heritage; Liz Multon and all the staff at Conway for having faith in me; and the Outdoor Writers and Photographers Guild for giving me the confidence and means to approach Conway with my idea.

ABOVE Goodrich Castle.